Once Through the NEW TESTAMENT

Once Through the NEW TESTAMENT

Thomas McCall and Zola Levitt

CHRISTIAN HERALD BOOKS
Chappaqua, New York

Library of Congress Cataloging in Publication Data

McCall, Thomas S.
  Once through the New Testament.

1. Bible. N.T. — Introductions.   I. Levitt.
Zola, joint author.   II.   Title.
BS2330.2.M2   225.6'1   80-69306
ISBN 0-915684-78-0 (pbk.)

Christian Herald, independent, evangelical and interdenominational, is dedi-cated to publishing wholesome, inspirational and religious books for Christian families.

 MEMBER OF
EVANGELICAL CHRISTIAN
PUBLISHERS ASSOCIATION

First Edition

CHRISTIAN HERALD BOOKS,
40 Overlook Drive,
Chappaqua, New York 10514
Printed in the United States of America

CONTENTS

Part I — The Story

1. When God Became Man 13
2. The Week That Was 27
3. The Unique Eternal Person 43
4. Every Nation Under Heaven
   (Acts).................................... 51
5. The New Message 71
   (Romans, Galatians, Thessalonians,
   Colossians, Philippians, and Philemon)
6. The New People 83
   (Ephesians, Corinthians)
7. The New Leaders 95
   (Timothy and Titus)
8. The New Jews 103
   (Hebrews, James, Peter)
9. The Enemy Within
   (John and Jude) 111
10. From Here to Eternity
   (Revelation) 117

Part 2 — The Continuing Drama

11. Prophecy Fulfilled 129
12. Prophecy Unfulfilled 137
13. The Development of Doctrine 145

Once Through the NEW TESTAMENT

Part I
The Story

1

When God Became Man

Presently we live in the strange stuff we call "time."
There wasn't always time. Time is a thing that separates eternity past, when God was alone, from eternity
future, when He will exist with certain parts of His creation.
Our time-bound, earth-bound minds wrestle hopelessly with
the picture of eternity past, when there were no worlds, no
creatures, no stars, no universe, no angels—nothing but
God. The Almighty was an only "Being"; He was all that
was, and within Him was the essence of such marvelous
attributes as light, life, and love, but these characteristics
were not shared with anything or anyone because nothing
other than God existed.

If God was totally alone then who is our reporter? How
do we know all this?

Our information comes from God's book, the Bible, in
which He has disclosed the essence of His history and character. Beginning in the Old Testament and continuing with
greater detail in the New Testament, God has chosen to
report upon Himself for our benefit. Other theories of our
origins outside of the biblical record inevitably leave us hun-
gry again. They all lack that majestic First Being. They all
picture an unliving, unloving commencement of the universe and our own lives, and they tend to leave us with
perplexing questions. The biblical version, if it is believed,
is infinitely more satisfying. It tells us not only of the past
but of the vast and timeless future. It describes that solitary
creating Being as our Father. It describes us as having a

place in His love and a fixed, predetermined place in His infinite creation.

He made us and He loves us; and so we are, and so we live.

The Eternal Christ

Our major interest in this book is the part of God we call Jesus Christ. Our one God describes Himself biblically as existing in three personalities, with inter-relationships defined in our terms as Father, Son, and Spirit. God is three persons in One, what theologians call the Trinity. While each of the three personalities is God Himself, containing all the divine attributes, they appear to have distinct areas of responsibility: the Father designs, the Son enacts, and the Spirit directs the resulting activity. The New Testament makes particularly clear that God is One, yet with three vital missions carrying forth through three separate personalities. The entirety of creation, with all its myriad activities and features, is directed with love, cohesiveness, order, and enormous power by the personalities of God.

As the story of the New Testament unfolds, the Son takes the leading role. We are told that the baby born in that obscure village of Bethlehem did not actually begin there— He is in fact the Son of God. Being the Son of God He had no beginning; He is eternal. He is part of the Triune God that has existed forever. In fact, we are told, the individual who occupied the body of the baby in the manger is the One who created the universe!

> All things were made by him; and
> without him was not anything made
> that was made (John 1:3).

Since our conception of Jesus arises from our position

in time—since we picture Him as a carpenter of Galilee who lived two thousand years ago—we have problems seeing Him as the Maker of the stars, the world, the animals, and us ourselves. But the Scripture is very clear; He is co-equal and co-eternal with the Father and the Spirit, and His particular role in the creation of the universe evidently was to enact the express will of the Father. Jesus brought all energy and matter into existence and arranged these elements in the forms that we now see them. How inconceivable a task, and how exquisitely He performed it!

But creation was not the only role of Jesus Christ. He also acts in the redemption of the human race. Before anything was created it was fully understood by God that humanity would desert Him and fall into rebellion. In the eternal counsel of deity it was also understood that the Son would set in motion a plan to redeem many descendants of Adam. The Son would become a human being Himself and demonstrate firsthand the nature of Almighty God, and finally and most importantly, offer Himself as an atonement for sin.

This was not done in only the short life-span of Jesus Christ as a human being but was prepared some millennia beforehand. Humanity in general, and the select nation of Israel in particular, were presented with the concept of redemption and reconciliation to God beginning with the Garden of Eden. Each human being was undeniably supplied with the concepts of good and evil and with the knowledge of what was God and what was not God. Men in their free will departed in many directions, but God's presence and His mercy were invariably available to them all.

At the right moment and in answer to much forecasting, the Son took the great leap of the Incarnation—He became purely a human being, His divine nature virtually hidden. Many who even met and talked with Him did not perceive His deity. They were free to do so or not do so, and Jesus gave just enough information about His special nature so that man's free choice was left intact.

The perceptive listener to Jesus Christ—the one who had "ears to hear"—could see deity in Him and true reconciliation to God. The one with little interest in God or His Word or His attributes seemed to see in Jesus nothing but human intellect, blasphemy, and danger to the state.

Nobody felt neutral about him.

Prophetic Puzzles

The arrival of Jesus Christ on the stage of world history was one of the most anticipated and predicted events, at least to those familiar with the Old Testament Scriptures. There were dozens of prophecies about the Messiah couched in most of the thirty-nine books of the Old Testament. Some of them very clear and others a bit more cryptic. A reasonable amount of biblical scholarship was necessary on the part of those who would see the Messiah come to authenticate that He was truly the expected One.

It is beyond our scope here to review the entire body of Messianic prophecy, but we will look into a few of those passages which show the evidence of divine intervention into the affairs of men. God seemed to have set Himself up a puzzling and subtle system of Messianic identification through certain prophecies that only He could fulfil. It seemed that those who would be faithful and apply themselves to serious study of God's Word would recognize Jesus as the promised Messiah by faith, while the casual and indifferent might altogether miss His coming through unfamiliarity with the prophecies.

Three particularly unique riddles of prophecy clearly show the intervention of the Divine Hand:

1. The Messiah was to be born in the obscure town of Bethlehem about five miles south of Jerusalem.
2. The Messiah was to be a descendant of King David and a legal heir to David's throne, but *not* a descendant of King Jeconiah, the last Davidic monarch in Israel's history.
3. The Messiah was to suffer and die, but He was also to reign forever.

The Gospel writers, especially Matthew, were intrigued by the way God handled the problems and paradoxes and fulfilled all of the prophecies so perfectly. The biblically-aware Israelite would look in vain for any Messianic prophecy that is not fulfilled in Jesus, but the three we have selected are among the most ingenious of God's outworkings. In discussing them below we will show that the Almighty went to considerable trouble to present His Son as announced.

"O Little Town..."

The problem with Bethlehem was that Christ's parents did not live there or anywhere near there. The prophet Micah had been very clear (Micah 5:2) in specifying this particular small village, but the chosen mother, Mary, and her husband, Joseph, lived in Nazareth, more than ninety miles away. Between Bethlehem and the Galilean town of Nazareth lay forbidding mountains and arid terrain, requiring a journey of many days by donkey. It was hardly an ideal situation for a teen-age girl about to give birth.

Only the most extraordinary circumstances would compel Joseph to undertake such an arduous journey at such a time, but the prophecy had to be fulfilled. If even one solitary Messianic prophecy remained unsatisfied, men could reject Jesus with authority even to this day. But in fact, the trip was made compulsory by the Roman rulers of Israel.

At just this time Emperor Caesar Augustus decided to take a thorough census of the people throughout the empire, including those in his far-flung province of Israel. The Romans had refined taxation to an art form, but in Israel they had the problem of people of various tribes moving about within the land so that they escaped the municipal rolls. Rather like in today's voter registrations, everyone had to make a journey to their ancestral town, or precinct, to register. Since Joseph and Mary were both descendants of King David of Bethlehem, they were obliged to obey this inconvenient governmental decree.

Thus the Emperor's unusual plan, Mary's full term pregnancy, the little town of Bethlehem, and Micah's prophecy all came together at one point in time and space so that the Messiah could be born exactly in accordance with God's previous announcement.

Jeconiah's Curse

The usual interpretation of the Virgin Birth (Isaiah 7:14) is that the Son of God had to be truly human (born of a woman) but not tainted with the seed of human sinfulness. True enough, but the Virgin Birth also fulfills one of those "impossible" conundrums of Messianic prophecy.

God had clearly stated that the Messiah had to be a physical descendant of King David (2 Samuel 7:12–13). However, the last divinely authorized descendant of David's dynasty to rule in Jerusalem was King Jeconiah. The youthful Jeconiah had inherited the unlucky situation of the invasion and destruction of the Temple by Nebuchadnezzar of Babylon. Just before he was carried off in captivity, God pronounced a curse on Jeconiah to the effect that none of his descendants would ever sit on the hallowed throne of David (Jeremiah 22:28–30).

Surely the Almighty had created a true impossibility this time. The promise to David and the curse upon Jeconiah simply would not match.

The solution to this dilemma lies in a careful comparison of the genealogies of Joseph and Mary as given in Matthew and Luke respectively. Joseph, we find, was of the cursed line of Jeconiah (interestingly, if Israel had still been a monarchy at the time, and if Jeconiah's curse had not been in effect, then Joseph, the carpenter of Nazareth, would have been the rightful King of Israel!) But Joseph was not a part of the birth of Jesus Christ. Due to the phenomenon of the Virgin Birth only Mary and God were concerned. Thus, by adoption, Joseph was able to pass on the legal right to the throne of Jesus without passing on the curse of the seed of Jeconiah. Mary, a descendant of King David through another line, which did not include Jeconiah and the royal dynasty, was able to pass on to Jesus the lineage of David apart from the curse. Thus we see that just the right earthly couple had to be selected by God so that all prophecy might be fulfilled and none violated. Joseph and Mary truly had to be the right people at the right place at the right time.

And those who looked deeply into the prophecies and curses of God could only marvel at how specifically the Almighty had identified His Son. We should appreciate that there have always been pretenders to the Messianic throne of Israel. The true Messiah had to have an absolutely specific descendency and utterly accurate scriptural sanctions.

Life After Death

The ancient rabbis were fully aware of the apparent contradiction between the prophecies that predicted the suffering and death of the Messiah and those that promised His kingship and eternal life. The Old Testament clearly speaks of both roles for the Messiah, and it is only with hindsight, we should realize, that the idea of His two comings becomes clear.

Jesus did demonstrate that His first coming was designed to be one of humility, suffering, sacrificial death, and resurrection. "For this was I born," He said, and, "This is my blood of the New Testament which is shed for many for the remission of sins." (He certainly did not fear death but chose it.) He gave His earthly life for the important purpose of standing in for all sinners of all times and accepting their penalty.

He did not begin to utilize His royal power, though His divine prerogatives were apparent in the miracles He performed; the world still awaits His second coming when the total promise of His eternal reign will be realized.

Those who today refuse the Messiah because He did not in fact ascend to the throne of Israel and the world, simply fail to see that this ultimate fulfillment could not be combined with His sacrificial mission. The return of Jesus Christ is the great promise of Christianity and Judaism. He is alive but temporarily departed. His promise as He left us was, "I go to prepare a place for you . . . If it were not so I would have told you" (see John 14:2).

"Never Man Spake Like This..."

He was the incomparable teacher of the masses of people. He addressed Himself to the ultimate questions of life and death in terms that no earthly philosopher would dare to approach. The crowds were constantly astonished, both by the content of what he said and the utter confidence with which He said it. Educators through the centuries have marveled at His skill in pedagogy.

The most brilliant minds in Israel—the priests at the Temple, the lawyers and the scriptural scholars—carped about His apparently humble origin and His less than kingly manner. But they were confounded by the impact of His pronouncements and the unfathomable depth of His speeches. Even the unbelieving philosophers of the ages have had to concede to Jesus the central role in the history of human thought. Far above the level of the highest order of human thinkers stands Jesus of Nazareth with his complete understanding of all things divine and worldly. His teachings cut to the heart of anyone exposed to them. The ideas once expressed to a handful of Galilean tradesmen have now become the dominant religion of the modern world.

We cannot treat the subjects of Jesus Christ in the space we have, and indeed, only the Gospels themselves adequately chronicle His masterful conceptions. The high points of the multitude of Jesus' subjects are the things He taught about His own nature, His kingdom, and His totally original policy of gracious forgiveness. With all due humility we will attempt to explain below the Master's thoughts on these three crucial and world-changing areas.

Jesus on Jesus

Jesus conveyed in no uncertain terms the information that He was in fact the Messiah, the unique Son of Man and Son of God, and the One who would ultimately judge all the thoughts and actions of all humanity. And yet He was able to communicate these unheard of claims—this unthinkable "blasphemy"—with stunning humility. It was the overwhelming force of His messages combined with the meekness of His manner that intrigued the crowds who hung on His every word. Often, rather than make claims for Himself, He elicited the Messianic convictions from those who came in contact with Him. He was a questioner of supreme intelligence who brought men's hearts and minds to the truth utterly without a self-aggrandizing word.

Rugged fishermen beached their boats and common laborers traveled all over Israel with Him to sit at His feet. The divine wisdom He uttered caused them finally to exclaim with Peter, "You are the Christ, the Son of the Living God!"

Such a character as the avaricious tax collector, Zachaeus, avowed that he would refund to anyone that he had cheated a proper recompense plus 400% interest! Zachaeus' encounter with the Son of God completely changed the man, and the effect is still apparent with men today. The Samaritan woman (John 4), with her mediocre reputation and outspoken ways, was transformed by Jesus Christ into an energetic evangelist. She approached the people of her town, Sychar, exclaiming that she had encountered the Messiah of Israel. She was a changed woman and she accounted for the salvation of many.

Invariably, the people who encountered Jesus Christ in person were truly reborn—no other term will suffice.

The lepers by the road, and even the occasional educated Pharisee (John 3), were utterly changed when they were exposed to the teaching of Christ about Himself. They were excited. They were convinced that He had a special claim upon their very lives. They were convinced that He was nothing short of God Himself Incarnate on earth.

Jesus on the Kingdom

But where was the kingdom promised to Israel?

Jesus began His ministry by saying, "The kingdom of heaven is at hand." That was the way in which He introduced His program for Israel and the world. It was a new order, not contradictory to the old order of the law of Moses, but fulfilling it and elevating it to a vastly broader spiritual plane. The King had finally come, after some two thousand years of promises since Abraham, and now He was able to present the nature of His kingdom to His subjects.

It was a kingdom that would be marked by the humility, faith, holiness, and forgiving posture of its King. It would be a voluntary kingdom; (each subject had to personally come forward and accept the King).

The earth has never seen the kind of kingdom offered by Jesus Christ because it was a kingdom of heaven. Things have never been "done on earth as they are in heaven" and thus men have no experience by which to estimate conditions in the kingdom. Other than for the idyllic descriptions of kingdom times by the Old Testament prophets, particularly Isaiah, a heavenly kingdom with a heavenly king, heavenly subjects, and heavenly principles is far beyond our view of things.

Earthly kingdoms are established by weapons and power politics; a heavenly kingdom is established by meekness and prayer.

Theological views about the kingdom proposed by Jesus Christ abound generously among Bible students. Our view is the so-called *Postponement Theory*, which teaches that the kingdom is yet to come, since Israel did not accept it. The Messianic millennial kingdom was announced to Israel in a bona fide offer, but the leadership of Israel and the majority of the people did not anticipate the terms given by the Messiah. Had Israel accepted the offer, human history would have been vastly altered. It is important to realize that the kingdom was not "canceled" but put off until the end of this age of salvation of the Gentiles. The millennial kingdom will be established in God's timing, in Israel, at the second coming of Christ.

Jesus continued to teach about the kingdom even after it became clear that Israel was not going to accept it. But His messages were subtly changed. The teaching began to refer not to the millennial kingdom with the Messiah ruling the world from Jerusalem, but a kingdom the Old Testament prophets knew nothing about—a kingdom that would exist between the two comings of the Messiah. The King would be away in heaven and His subjects would struggle in a world of good and evil until His return. A major feature of this inter-advent kingdom would be the institution called the Church, the *ekklesia*, the "called out group." And so the Church, the Jewish and Gentile believers in Jesus Christ, exists as a kind of preview of the greater millennial kingdom to come.

This view clarifies apparently contradictory statements about the nature of the kingdom that are made throughout the Gospels. "We have the kingdom in part," some say, accurately enough, but we of course look forward to much greater days to come.

"Forgive Them, Father..."

Jesus Christ forgave everyone, even the soldiers who crucified Him, and the theme of forgiveness recurs constantly
throughout His discourses. He alone in human history *could*
forgive sin, and He did so graciously. There would come
a day, He gave fair warning, in which He would judge the
world, but not for the moment. "Now is the day of salvation"
(2 Cor. 6:2). In this age God is forgiving sin wholesale, and
Jesus truly enjoyed teaching about that forgiveness.

The Messiah told eloquently about the runaway son who
returned to his father's open arms, the servant who had
been forgiven an enormous debt by his employer, and the
woman caught in adultery, whom He did not condemn. He
stressed that those who had been forgiven by God should
in turn be forgiving toward their fellow men. He heaped
scathing rebuke on the servant who had his own great debt
canceled but refused to forget the small debt someone else
owed him. He taught us to ask our Father in heaven to
"forgive us as we forgive those who trespass against us."
If we wish to come to the very heart and soul of the teachings
of Jesus Christ, we must understand this total forgiveness,
this overwhelming compassion, this amazing grace.

Signs and Wonders

The Messiah would be a miracle worker, the Old Testament prophets said, and Jesus indeed accomplished many
great wonders as a testimony of His Messiahship. To John
the Baptist's query he replied:

> Go your way, and tell John what things
> ye have seen and heard; how that the

blind see, the lame walk, the lepers
are cleansed, the deaf hear, the dead
are raised, to the poor the gospel
is preached (Luke 7:22).

It is significant that the healings of Jesus were achieved
with those whose ailments were well established. We cannot
patronize the Gospel stories with accusations of "psycho-
somatic healings" or cures of mere hysteria. Jesus Christ
was deeply compassionate toward the sick, but He also used
His healing power to authenticate His teachings and to
underline the idea that He was indeed the Messiah, able to
cure the incurable.

His miracles were not limited to healings, of course. He
walked on the Sea of Galilee, calmed the dangerous storm
and allowed His Deity to shine forth at the Transfiguration.
Calmly, and with His characteristic humility, He even raised
the dead!

It seemed that the miracles were in the service of identifying the Messiah rather than merely enthralling His audiences or combatting those who doubted Him.

We apologize for the brevity of our remarks concerning
so magnificent a subject. There is no good book about the
New Testament that is not many times as long and cum-
bersome as the original text, and our space is quite a bit
more limited than that. Our purpose, to show how Jesus
Christ's birth, teachings and miracles evidenced that unique
combination of God and man the prophets clearly specified
to Israel, limits our treatment. We thus press on with our
all-too-sketchy explanations of the person of Jesus Christ,
cautioning the reader to consult the original, since that is the
actual record given us by the Holy Spirit.

2

The Week That Was

One-third of all the writing of the Gospels describes Jesus' final week.

The four Gospels cover in detail His birth and His dramatic three years of public ministry. But fully thirty chapters out of the eighty-nine momentously report the events of that ultimate week of crucifixion and resurrection. Apparently of more crucial importance than the establishment of His Deity, Messiahship, and the authority of His teachings was the drama wrought at the end—the week surrounding the Lord's final Passover.

"This is My Blood"

Ten years ago a controversial book entitled *The Passover Plot* received wide acclaim. The author pointed out the remarkably detailed interrelationship between the death of Jesus and the feast of Passover. His theory was that Jesus conspired with His associates to have Himself arrested and appear to die at just that highly significant moment. We can appreciate the author's recognition of the vital importance of Passover in the sacrificial death of Christ, but obviously this death was not the result of any human conspiracy. The crucifixion of the one called the Lamb of God, at just the time when His nation was celebrating its liberation from bondage in Egypt during the time of Moses, was a divinely-orchestrated masterpiece.

We should realize that the assassination of Jesus Christ

was attempted previous to this Passover season. On at least two occasions there were efforts to arrest Him, but they were unsuccessful. Not that Jesus was so elusive a desperado; the Scriptures comment simply that "his hour was not yet come" (John 7:30; 8:20). But on Passover Eve of that fateful year, Jesus told His disciples, "I have desired to eat this passover with you before I suffer" (Luke 22:15). During the feast that night He spoke of the deep truths about His sacrifice the next day and established the taking of the bread and wine "in remembrance of me." Jesus' discourses before, during, and after the Passover meal reached new levels of subtlety and majesty. His disciples' eyes were opened to the magnificent depth and breadth of His entire mission. They and the rest of the world would never be the same.

Actually, Jesus formally came into Jerusalem four days before Passover, on the tenth day of the month of Nisan. This Sunday, now known as Palm Sunday, was the appropriate day for Him to appear as the sacrificial lamb so that He might be examined by the people as to His suitability as a sacrifice. Exodus 12:3–6 discloses that God wanted the Hebrew people to take the sacrificial lamb four days before the feast and inspect it for "blemishes" before they actually offered it. Thus Jesus, in an obvious repeat performance of that first Passover, presented Himself riding into the East Gate of Jerusalem on a donkey four days before the feast.

It was a dramatic and dangerous moment. Jesus was not welcome in Jerusalem, at least not by the ruling powers, and yet the people waved palm branches and many praised Him aloud shouting, "Hosannah!" ("Save us"). Many present understood that this event was the fulfillment of Zechariah's pronouncement concerning the future King of the Jews:

> Rejoice greatly, O daughter of Zion;
> shout, O daughter of Jerusalem: behold,
> thy King cometh unto thee: he is just,

and having salvation; lowly, and riding
upon an ass, and upon a colt the foal
of an ass (Zechariah 9:9).

The temple priesthood and authorities were not nearly
as impressed as the people at large. They advised Jesus
straightforwardly to hush up the people's adulation. He replied, however, that there was no way to cover up the
coming of the King. If the people were silenced, He said,
the very stones would begin to cry out (Luke 19:40). The
peaceful hillside of the Mount of Olives, lying just adjacent
to the eastern wall of the Temple site, had thus become a
scene of salvation for the accepting Jewish pilgrims, and
one of consternation for the objecting Pharisees.

And so that final week had begun.

Over the next few days Jesus spoke in public in the
Temple, disregarding the obvious peril. We must appreciate
that to be in Jerusalem at Passover in that time was to join
some three million worshipers from a wide variety of surrounding lands who had come to the Holy City to celebrate
the ancient feast. The Temple site occupies thirty-four
acres—perhaps the size of a modern sports stadium; but no
sports stadium can accommodate three million people. Jesus seized upon the occasion of this enormous gathering of
Israelites and made it the platform for the proclamation of
His Messiahship and His redemptive sacrifice.

The Teacher from the provinces was absolutely fearless.
Observed by the huge crowds, He strode up to the massive
enclosure on the Temple Mount and began throwing over
the exchange tables of the businessmen who changed the
money of the foreign pilgrims. It was not the presence of
the money changers—they were a necessity—but the ex-
orbitant commissions they extracted that infuriated Jesus.
He was angered that this sort of avarice went on within the
confines of the sanctuary of God. In righteous wrath, the
Messiah chased out of the Temple the mercenaries, making

His feelings very clear—"My father's house shall be called the house of prayer" (Matthew 21:13).

If anyone had been ignorant of the presence of Christ in Jerusalem, or had purposely tried to avoid Him, it was now impossible to do so. We can well imagine the reaction of the stunned crowds at the courage and the obvious sincerity of convictions, of this one-of-a-kind holy Man. For Jesus' part, He had taken center stage and was determined to press His claims before the people to the fullest, knowing clearly the destiny that awaited Him at the end of that week.

Perhaps in the day of judgment many will say, "I didn't see Him come," but they will not be among those who attended that particular Passover.

David's Lord

The content of Jesus' teaching was explosive. He told the multitude in the Temple, His disciples on the Mount of Olives, and even the opposing authorities when they challenged Him, that He was the promised King, the Messiah. He had been more reticent before that time, but He now made full disclosure in the plainest terms, openly declaring His divine heritage and bringing all discussion of the matter to an absolute conclusion.

To the contentious Temple leadership, He revealed that the Messiah was not only to be human but also divine:

> While the Pharisees were gathered together,
> Jesus asked them,
>
> Saying, What think ye of Christ? whose
> son is he? They say unto him, The son
> of David.

He saith unto them, How then doth David
in spirit call him Lord, saying,

The Lord said unto my Lord, Sit thou on
my right hand, till I make thine enemies
thy footstool?

If David then call him Lord, how is
he his son?

And no man was able to answer him a
word, neither durst any man from that
day forth ask him any more questions
(Matthew 22:41–46).

It was hopeless to argue with Jesus, the skeptical ones
well knew. They had always regarded that He was simply
too clever for them, but now He was teaching new truths
from Scripture in which they were learned. And His argument was compelling. If the Messiah was merely David's
son, why then did the powerful King David refer to Him as
his Lord? If the Messiah were to be merely a man, why
would one in David's position pay Him such obeisance?
The answer, of course, had to do with Jesus' lineage as the
Son of God as well as the son of David, and it was this
rightful claim to deity that led the Pharisees to accuse Him
of the capital crime of blasphemy.

The Last Supper

From reading the record one could get the feeling that
if the period between Jesus' triumphal entry and the actual
Passover meal were any longer than four days He never
would have made it! It was certainly a tumultuous time of

confrontation between Christ and the leadership of Israel, and the devastating reaction of the leadership was now only a matter of time.

It was hardly a situation of one man against the nation. The cause of gravest concern on the part of the Temple authorities was that many of Jesus' countrymen were following Him. It is casually assumed that all Israel rejected Jesus Christ, but if that were true there would have been no cause for concern. Rather, as in that overwhelming triumph on Palm Sunday, many Jewish people examined their Lamb and accepted Him as their sacrifice.

With the coming of Passover Eve, Jesus told His disciples to make the appropriate preparations. These included their selecting of a suitable lamb, taking it to the Temple for sacrifice, offering a portion on the altar, and bringing the remainder to the Upper Room on Mount Zion for the meal.

Jesus went through the various ordinances of the ancient feast, dipping the unleavened bread and giving it to Judas with the instruction that he do his work quickly.

Judas, like all Israel, has been accused of the death of Christ, but more likely the crucifixion surprised him. Despite his three-year association with Jesus, his concept of the Messiah was completely at variance with what the Master was doing and teaching. He understood only, and probably more quickly and deeply than the other disciples, that Jesus was on a collision course with the government, and he may have acted out of a patriotic motive, protecting Israel from Rome. The thirty pieces of silver answer to his worldliness, but he might have thought that the apprehension of Jesus would be for the good of his country, and possibly for the Master's own protection. He may have assumed that Jesus would only be discredited, reprimanded, and imprisoned. After the verdict of condemnation, however, Judas realized the awesomeness of his crime and committed suicide. This is not to excuse Judas, who allowed himself to be used by

Satan, but to show the want of understanding of the earth-bound human heart. In any case, Judas fulfilled the prophecy that one of the Messiah's own friends would betray Him (Psalm 41:9; John 13:18).

After Judas' departure Jesus continued the Passover ceremony, washing His disciples' feet in exemplary humility, and explaining the elements of the feast in its commemoration of the redemption of Israel out of Egypt. But when He came to the traditional *matzah*, the unleavened bread, and the wine, He gave them startling new significance. The "bread of affliction," baked by the Hebrew slaves as they hastened out of Egypt, now symbolized the broken body of the Messiah. The red wine, which commemorated the redemption from Egypt through the blood of the Passover lamb, now signified the blood to be shed by the Messiah "for the remission of sins." The ceremony of the bread and wine was henceforth not to be done in remembrance of the exodus from Egypt; Jesus now said, "Do this in remembrance of me."

Many other fundamental truths of the faith were uttered in the Lord's overwhelming Upper Room discourse. (John 13–17). The Master disclosed His imminent departure but informed His disciples that he would return:

> Let not your heart be troubled: ye
> believe God, believe also in me.

> In my Father's house are many mansions:
> if it were not so, I would have told you.
> I go to prepare a place for you.

> And if I go and prepare a place for you,
> I will come again, and receive you unto
> myself; that where I am, there ye may be
> also (John 14:1–3).

Therein lies the difference between Christianity and the worldly religions.

The Lord also said, "I and the Father are one," and promised the coming of the Holy Spirit. He said, "Peace I give unto you." He said, "These things I command you, that ye love one another." He warned the disciples of persecution in the world, and He disclosed the enabling work of the Holy Spirit to come. He spoke of His death, resurrection and second advent, and finally closed with a majestic prayer of intercession.

The Garden Arrest

The disciples listened in awestruck silence as they followed the Lord to the Garden of Gethsemane, near the East Gate of the Temple. Jesus well knew what was coming, but His men seemed to have only a vague comprehension that this was indeed the night of the sacrifice of the Lamb.

The peace and beauty of the quiet olive orchard outside of the bustling festival city belied the immense spiritual battle taking place within the heart of Jesus Christ that night. With the heavy weight of all the past and future sins of the human race crushing His spirit, and Satan doing all within his terrifying power to dissuade the human Jesus from going through with the ordeal of the sacrifice, the Lord consulted His Father. Jesus would rather have not gone to the cross we learn from the record (Luke 22:39–42). "Let this cup pass from me," He said. But His obedience to the will of His Father surpassed His aversion. The Almighty God encouraged His Son and reinforced the eternally understood agreement that there was no way that the cup of atoning death could be bypassed if there were to be salvation for a lost and dying human race.

We can well understand the horror with which Jesus faced the specter of physical death and execution. But what we may never understand is the torture of His having to be consigned to hell in our place. In those odious hours on the cross He would be separated, for the first time in all eternity, from the Father, while taking upon Himself the awful guilt and punishment of our sin and rebellion against God. We who spend most of our lives outside of fellowship with God can scarcely enter into the agony of Christ as He wrestled with those realities in the Garden.

We are in a position to know about men dying in agony because we have seen that. We are in no position to contemplate God dying in agony.

Jesus sweated drops of blood while His well-meaning friends slept and while the authorities in Jerusalem dispatched a detachment of police with Judas for the arrest of Jesus Christ. Over thirty thousand angels ("twelve legions") were standing by to protect the Lord at His request, we learn in the record, but that request never came. The Son of God chose instead to lay down His life for His friends.

The police came in force, as if to confront a dangerous and desperate outlaw, but they had little trouble arresting Jesus Christ. Judas identified His Master with an oriental kiss on the cheek, and the Lord was led away to the first of His two trials. His disciples ran off in every direction, confused and afraid.

God Judged

The One who taught all men to "judge not" was taken before both Jewish and Gentile authorities. In the end, the answer to "who killed Christ?" is "All of us," through our various representatives at those trials.

Jesus was sentenced to death in both courts. His crime

before the Jewish Sanhedrin was blasphemy, since He had declared He was the Messiah. Before the Roman court it was insurrection, because He dared to proclaim Himself king in defiance of Caesar. Obviously neither the Jewish nor the Gentile worlds could tolerate the existence of the Galilean, and they thought execution would be the most expedient way to rid themselves of Him. How clearly John saw that there was no place for Christ either in Israel or abroad, even though He had created the world and had come to His own people: He was in the world, and the

> world was made by him, and the world knew him not.
>
> He came unto his own, and his own
> received him not (John 1:10-11).

Some teach that Jesus was just a misunderstood religious reformer and never claimed to be the Messiah or a king. If that had been the case, He would never have been put to death. Before the Sanhedrin all sorts of accusations were brought against Jesus, but He remained utterly silent, apparently unwilling to discuss matters lesser than His claim to be the very Son of God. But when the High priest in exasperation asked the fateful question point-blank, Jesus was very clear:

> Art thou the Christ, the Son of the
> Blessed? (Mark 14:61).
>
> And Jesus said, "I am" (Mark 14:62).

Moreover, the Lord went on in His answer to say "and ye shall see the Son of man sitting on the right hand of power, and coming in the clouds of heaven" (Mark 14:62). This unmistakable reference to Messianic prophecy and the Lord's outright declaration of His Messiahship caused pandemonium in the courtroom. It had been the right question from the right person at the right time in the right place, and Jesus now dropped His posture of silence and declared with all possible force the statement that condemned Him to death. Without stopping to evaluate the truthfulness of Jesus' startling claim, Caiaphas and the Sanhedrin declared the Lord a blasphemer and sealed His death warrant.

However, it should be realized that the Jews could not execute Jesus or anyone else. A short time before, Rome had removed the power of capital punishment from occupied Israel. This seemed to be only a temporary prohibition because not much later, the deacon Stephen was executed by stoning under the authority of the Sanhedrin (Acts 7:58, 8:1). Apparently, for a relatively brief time Israel could not conduct executions, and the time of the Lord's trial came in that period. It was as though God had arranged that Israel was not to bear the sole burden for the death of Christ, but rather it was to be shared by the Gentile world in the form of Rome. Two thousand years of accusations singling out the Jews as "Christ killers" have no basis in legal fact. Without Roman participation the Lord simply could not have been executed in Israel at that time.

And thus we have the reason for the second trial, the one before the Roman court. The procurator, Pontius Pilate, officiated personally although he had to be persuaded to do so. He seemed to have no hostility toward Jesus nor any interest in the theological tangles that attended the accusations against Him. Finally convinced that the process of keeping the peace in Jerusalem involved an investigation of the Galilean preacher, Pilate held a brief hearing aimed at examining Christ's claims to be king. Blasphemy, of course, had no meaning in that secular court, but the Roman occupation would not permit the existence of any sort of king in Israel. Thus it was finally Caesar and Caesar's authority that condemned Jesus Christ on that day.

Pilate had some difficulty perceiving just what his defendant was king of; the Galilean clearly stated that He was a king, but that His kingdom was "not of this world." All the same, if this man Jesus were ever acknowledged as a king by the population of Israel there would be a problematical situation with regard to the Roman emperor. Without much conviction then, Pilate ordered Jesus Christ to be slain by crucifixion.

Both the Jews and the Romans were, of course, acting in perfect accordance with God's plan. Neither court even entertained the idea that the claims of Jesus were true, but they were both ignorant of the real nature of the case. They simply did not connect the Galilean carpenter with either the Son of God or the coming King of this world. Both plaintiffs in the case saw only potential trouble and dealt with it harshly.

And in doing so, they fulfilled God's will.

The Cross

And so it was that Jesus died on Passover Day. In a more cosmic way, He was, of course, the Lamb of God "slain from the foundation of the world" (Revelation 13:8) who died for reasons unfathomable to the people of the time. But just as the original Passover lamb back in Egypt provided the blood that spared the lives of the Israelites, so the blood of Christ provides eternal life for us all. As a principle in either Testament, the blood of the lamb grants redemption from bondage.

Reams of literature have been written about the cross by biblical and medical scholars. Crucifixion is one of the cruellest forms of execution ever devised by man. It combines public humiliation, lingering agony, excruciating pain, exposure, loss of blood, dehydration, and suffocation. It was worthy of the depraved ingenuity of Roman statecraft.

Jesus' physical suffering on the cross was obvious. He cried out at one point, "I thirst!" (John 19:28). As His human body lay exposed to the sun and the elements it became completely dehydrated, and as the Psalmist declared, "my tongue cleaveth to my jaws" (Psalm 22:15). The enormous effort involved in heaving the body up to breathe adequately in such a position caused the victim to suffocate slowly on the cross. Normally, the condemned one had to push himself up by his nailed feet to relieve the strain on his chest, and this hopelessly agonizing process could go on by the day and night. Often the soldiers would break the legs of the crucified ones with iron bars so that they could no longer push themselves up and would expire more quickly. But this was not done in the case of Jesus, since by the time that mercy was to be extended He was already dead.

Greater than His physical suffering was His spiritual suffering on the cross. As the Lord had anticipated with genuine dread, He was separated from the Father for six hours, from 9 a.m. to 3:00 p.m. on Passover Day, as the sins of the whole world were charged to Him. What a hideous day for the Son of God! But was it really only a day from His perspective?

> But, beloved, be not ignorant of this
> one thing, that one day is with the
> Lord as a thousand years, and a thousand
> years as one day (2 Peter 3:8).

Was Christ on the cross a thousand years?

His spiritual suffering was evidenced by the anguished outcry, "My God, my God, why hast thou forsaken me?" The vastness of His separation from the Father is driven home to us. The plaintive cry quotes the twenty-second Psalm, one of the most remarkable of all the Messianic prophecies in the Old Testament. The Psalm is ascribed to King David, who lived a thousand years before Christ, and many centuries before crucifixion in all its misery was ever imagined. Yet the psalmist describes death by crucifixion in considerable detail, and the verses are written in the first person so that we may actually enter into the mind of Christ and suffer with Him as He died for us.

After His seven overwhelming pronouncements from the cross, the encouragement of the repentant thief hanging beside Him, the fulfillments of Isaiah 53 and Psalm 22, the darkening of the sky and the rumbling earthquake, and the splitting of the Temple veil as the Priest was officiating at the golden altar (Matthew 27:51), Jesus Christ died. His final words were, "It is finished."

His lifeless body was turned over to His friends since the Sabbath Eve was approaching, and they wrapped the corpse in linen cloth and laid it in the donated tomb of the affluent Joseph of Arimathea. Thus Christ was buried on the Feast of Unleavened Bread, the eve following Passover, fulfilling so beautifully His image as the "bread of life." The Lord had now fulfilled the first two Jewish holy feasts, each in the appropriate way, being crucified on Passover and buried on the day of the Feast of Unleavened Bread (Leviticus 23:5–6).

"He is Risen"

The third Jewish feast was First Fruits, which we now call Easter, and was prescribed to be the Sunday during the week of Unleavened Bread (Leviticus 23:11–12). On that morning after the Sabbath, a priest would take a sheaf of the first fruits from the barley harvest and wave it in front of the Temple in thanksgiving to God.

The dead Jesus Christ celebrated this feast too, and in a most remarkable way! He became the first fruits of those who will rise from the dead (1 Corinthians 15:22–23).

As the priest was waving the prescribed first fruits in the Temple, some grief-stricken women were approaching the tomb of Jesus Christ to administer the funeral preparations that had been interrupted by the Sabbath on the afternoon He died. But the vault stone had been moved, and they were told that He had risen from the dead. The Lord had celebrated the third feast, then, in its appropriate manner, becoming Himself the first fruits of God's great harvest of resurrections to come. He even made the proper offering; Matthew 27:52–53 shows that a number of other people were raised from the dead at that time. They were apparently Jesus' offering to the Father.

It would be far more biblical to call the resurrection day First Fruits than Easter, which was derived from the pagan goddess, Ishtar. Jesus was the first man permanently resurrected—that is, brought forth in a new resurrection body, unlike Lazarus and the others who died again. All who trust in Christ will experience this ultimate and permanent resurrection, "every man in his own order" (1 Cor. 15:23). Evidently we all have a number and Christ's number was one. "The dead in Christ will rise first," since they obviously have lower numbers. If we use the term *First* Fruits, then we can more easily imagine a second, third, fourth, and so on, and picture not just His resurrection but our own to come.

Despite the Lord's teachings and promises, the disciples were frightened and dispirited. They huddled together, incredulous as to the news that their crucified Master was genuinely alive again. But He appeared among them with "flesh and bones" in His resplendent resurrection body (Luke 24:39). Numerous times during the course of the next forty days, He showed them "with many infallible proofs" that He had indeed risen from the dead. He proceeded to teach them extensively about Himself and the Kingdom from the Old Testament Scriptures, the only existing Bible.

On the fortieth day He gathered the disciples on the summit of the Mount of Olives overlooking Jerusalem. He instructed them to go down into the city and pray, and to wait for the promise of the Father. When the Spirit of God came upon them they were to preach His Gospel to Israel and the whole world (Acts 1:9).

Thus ended the earthly ministry of the most unique man to ever walk among us. Before the astonished disciples He ascended into heaven, where He would remain until His promised return. It was surely the most remarkable three years the world had ever seen, and it resulted in a permanent change of history.

We do not see Him now, but we continually see the results of the new intercessory phase of His ministry, which He has continued until the present, from His position at the right hand of the Father in heaven.

The Unique Eternal Person

J ust as we are continually apologizing about the inadequacy of our estimations of Jesus Christ, so did the gospel writer, John:

> And there are also many other things
> which Jesus did, the which, if they
> should be written every one, I suppose
> that even the world itself could not
> contain the books that should be
> written (John 21:25).

With John, we have had to be very selective about the ministry of our Lord, and if this shortcoming causes readers to refer to the Gospels for verification and more learning, we have accomplished our purpose.

The Incomparable Christ

The difficulty in writing about Jesus Christ is, of course, that He is not comparable with earthbound philosophers or teachers, or even prophets, priests, or kings, for that matter—He is God. We cannot enter into His deity, omniscience, omnipotence, and sinlessness with any real understanding. These are His eternal attributes, and we can only speculate, with wonder, about their full meanings.

But then again, He was also fully a human being, and in this respect He is different from the Father and the Holy Spirit. Those two persons of the Godhead do not know experientially what it means to be imprisoned in human flesh and mind, to suffer emotionally and physically, and to die. The Son did all these things, but we can make only the poorest sort of comparisons with our own humanity when we are speaking of the Son of God.

The Only Mediator

The experience of the Son in being both God and man provides the human race with the only adequate mediator between us and the Father. We human beings have a representative in the Deity, and Deity has a representative in the human race:

For there is one God, and one mediator
between God and men, the man Christ
Jesus (1 Timothy 2:5).

Every religion proclaims mediation between man and God, and we have seen a host of prophets and sages of all stripes come forward to provide for men a line of communication to God. But all of those were born here, among men, and could rightfully claim no meaningful relationship to God. They might aspire by dint of good works or meditation or sensitivity or intelligence to claim a form of godliness, but obviously, so unlike Jesus, they have no intimate relationship with the Father. They may tell us that they know the way to the Father, or how to please the Father, but Jesus could say, "If you have seen me you have seen the Father" (John 14:9).

Jesus can fully represent humanity to Deity and *vice-versa*. It would be marvelous if management and labor, or some government and its populace, enjoyed such an effective mediator. Even the angels can scarcely comprehend this mediation arrangement—they have no such interrelationship with God. None of the other created entities have this relationship either; only God and the human race through Jesus Christ.

The early Christian theologians were confounded by the unique human-divine personality of Christ but finally developed the understanding from Scripture of what is known as the hypostatic union. Christ is simply one Person with two natures, which means that He is fully human and fully divine, and these two natures are eternally fused in the one Person of the Son.

Prophet, Priest, and King

Actually, the offices of prophet, priest, and king, as created in the Old Testament by divine decree, helped explain to Israel and the world the ultimate functions of the Son. His mediatorship clearly answers to the type, or illustration, in the Old Testament of the priest.

The Levitical Priest held the office of mediator between God and man, and offered the sacrifices and prayers from earth to God in heaven. He received in return propitiation and atonement from God for his creatures. This made a comprehensible example for the writer of Hebrews to seize upon the prophecy that the Messiah would serve as a priestly mediator (Psalms 110:4; Hebrews 5:6). The entire book of Hebrews, written to those with a true appreciation of the need of a mediator between earth and heaven, revolves around the priestly prophecy and develops the many facets of that office of Christ. The Messiah, the record states, is in fact the perfect priest, who simultaneously can combine all the power of God with total compassion for human frailty. It is significant that the generation after the resurrection saw the removal of the Temple from Jerusalem by the Romans and the complete cessation of all sacrificial worship on the part of Israel. It was as if God was clearly saying that the Old Testament mediator would no longer be effective since He had now sent His own more perfect version.

As a prophet, the Lord was something really special. The Old Testament prophets were sent by God to bring God's message to man. Jesus is the supreme Prophet because He not only *brought* God's message, but he *was* the message. John refers to Him as simply "The Word":

> In the beginning was the Word, and the
> Word was with God, and the Word was God
> (John 1:1).

Jesus prophesied indeed, foretelling the destruction of the Temple, the nature of the inter-advent Kingdom, the signs of the end of the age, and of His coming. But He differed from the previous prophets in that He Himself was the substance of all of these things to come. The Old Testament prophets foresaw the future; Jesus *is* the future.

The kingly ministry of the Lord has barely been manifested since its full realization will be involved with His second advent. True, He was received as King by those who waved the palm branches on the Mount of Olives, and He is King in the hearts of us who have received Him as such. He was crowned and mockingly inscribed as "King of the Jews" by His Roman executioners. But His true kingly functions await His role of King of Kings and Lord of Lords in future times (Revelation (19:16).

Just as surely as He was and is a prophet and priest, so in the end He will be King.

The kings in the Old Testament showed a rather uneven record of success. The lives of the venerable David and Solomon were shot through with debilitating sin, and often corruption leveled the throne of Israel as it does the ruling houses of so many nations today. The world will be much refreshed by a sinless and incorruptible King, and it is for this we pray, "Thy kingdom come, they will be done on earth as it is in heaven."

Four Views of Four Gospels

As one reads the four Gospel accounts, it becomes apparent that the four writers, Matthew, Mark, Luke, and John, wrote with different perspectives and purposes, though they chronicled the same Person and many of the same events. Each writer provides a somewhat different view of Christ. Matthew was inspired to write about Jesus as the Messiah of Israel, the fulfillment of the Old Testament prophecies. He quotes more of the Messianic prophecies than any of the other writers and draws many analogies between Christ and Israel, Christ and King David, and Christ and Moses. His Gospel also stresses the royal nature of Christ and develops the theme of the King and His Kingdom more than the other Gospels.

Mark wrote with more brevity and concentrated on Jesus as the Servant of the Lord. This is a major theme of the book of Isaiah; the prophet viewed both Israel and the Messiah as the Servant of the Lord. There is more reportage on the actions and miracles of Jesus in the Gospel of Mark than about His teachings. He is seen moving from one activity to another, consistently doing the works of His Father.

Luke portrays Jesus the man. The writer was a physician, and the humanness of Christ seems to have highly impressed him. He must have spent many hours with Mary, talking with her about the phenomenal events surrounding the announcement and birth of the Messiah and how these events affected her and Joseph. None of the other writers went into such detail about the angelic announcement to Mary and the miraculous birth. It is to Luke that we owe our marvelous Christmas stories. Luke also quoted Jesus' touching story of the prodigal son, and the account of the rich man and Lazarus that pulled back the curtain of life after death. Luke also stressed the universality of Christ— that His message was for all nations. He was to continue this reportage as a chronicler of the early church in the Book of Acts, which he also authored.

John, the last of the Gospel writers, took on the formidable task of contemplating Jesus as God manifest in the flesh. He was filled with wonder that Almighty God, Creator of all things, would come down to earth as one of us. His Gospel differs also from the others in that he did not try to present a chronological account of events as the other three, called the synoptic Gospels. He was very close to Jesus personally and wrote of himself as "the disciple whom Jesus loved" (John 21:7). John described Jesus in terms of the Word of God, the Word made flesh, the "only begotten Son":

> For God so loved the world, that he
> gave his only begotten Son, that
> whosoever believeth in him should not
> perish, but have everlasting life
> (John 3:16).

It was the Diety of Christ, then, that was paramount in John's thinking as he composed his beautiful account.

Thus the four writers depicted Jesus respectively as King Messiah, the Lord's Servant, the Son of Man, and the Son of God. Their concepts were not mutually exclusive since all four writers overlap somewhat in their characterizations of the Lord. But the above distinctions explain the major thrust of each writer.

If the Gospels alone constituted the New Testament we would have the important information that the human race was visited by God in the person of Jesus Christ. And we would realize that the world has never been the same since.

We would all marvel that those in Israel saw Him, heard Him, conversed with Him, observed His death, resurrection and ascension back to heaven, and we might act accordingly.

But the New Testament goes on, showing very candidly just how people acted in Israel and the other nations in response to the stunning revelations of the Apostles. The scripture writers went on, as in the Gospels, to record a remarkable variety of responses to the impact of God's sojourn among men.

We turn now to the hopes and dreams, the triumph and the turmoil of first-century Christianity, probably the most highly examined and discussed period in the history of man.

4

"Every Nation Under Heaven" (Acts)

I t is basically a tale of two apostles, Peter and Paul. They ministered to the Jews and Gentiles, respectively, and they changed Christianity from a sect of Judaism to a world-wide faith.

Without the Book of Acts, or the actions of the apostles, we would never comprehend how or why the gospel of the Israeli carpenter traveled from Jerusalem to the far corners of the Roman Empire. Acts shows a metamorphosis: it begins with the little group of disciples huddled around the Lord asking only if the Kingdom is soon to come, and it ends with installations called churches, led by pastors, elders and deacons, established almost everywhere in the known world. A band of twelve wanted men becomes an army of evangelists, and complete strangers to faith in one God become zealous Christians in the course of this book.

Peter and Paul

The two chief apostles of the infant church had clearly defined divisions of responsibility, as Paul explains:

> But contrariwise, when they saw that
> the gospel of the uncircumcision was
> committed unto me, as the gospel of
> the circumcision was unto Peter;

(For he that wrought effectually in
Peter to the apostleship of the circumcision, the same was mighty in me toward
the Gentiles:)

And when James, Cephas, and John, who
seemed to be pillars, perceived the
grace that was given unto me, they gave
to me and Barnabas the right hands of
fellowship; that we should go unto the
heathen, and they unto the circumcision (Galatians 2: 7–9).

Peter was to concentrate on continuing to take the gospel
to the Jewish people ("circumcision") in Israel and the dispersion, while Paul was to go to the Gentiles ("uncircum-
cision"). These responsibilities were not mutually exclusive
since Peter led Gentiles to Christ (Acts 10) and Paul was
most active in evangelizing the Jews (Acts 17: 1–4).

This distribution of mission strategy might seem strange
since Jewish people probably made up less than 1% of the
world's population, as they do today. Therefore, one apostle
was responsible for that minute number while the other was
to look after more than 99% of the people. But this was
God's plan. If the gospel were to go out to the whole world
the Jewish people had to be reached first (Romans 1:16).
Israel was the nation that had the Bible, the Messianic hope,
the covenant relationship with the Father, and the experience of conducting meaningful worship of the one true God.
Also, the Jewish people were now not only found in the
land of Israel but strategically scattered in cities throughout
the Roman Empire.

We can appreciate the difficulty faced by the various
apostles in Gentile lands. They brought the unknown Old
Testament to people who had no knowledge of prophecy
and who were not waiting for a Messiah. They confronted

pagans of every sort, many of whom were hostile to the message of salvation, and they spoke of a Creator God simply unknown to their audiences.

They could not conceivably have achieved their goal without the enabling power of the promised Comforter, the Holy Spirit.

"The Spirit Gives Life"

God found an ingenious way to witness to the Jews first and yet still send the Gospel to many lands. Jesus had ascended to His Father after a last encouragement to His followers (Acts 1:9–11). As the Feast of Pentecost approached, the disciples awaited the Holy Spirit.

We know how long they waited. Since the Lord had risen on the Feast of First Fruits and remained with them forty days, there remained ten days before the Festival of the Harvest, or Pentecost, which was specified to be fifty days after First Fruits (Leviticus 23:15–16). During those ten days they waited in prayer, selected a replacement for Judas and studied the Scriptures to anticipate what might happen next. There was no discouragement among them now, as there had been on that terrifying night of the crucifixion. They had seen Jesus Christ in His resurrected glory and their boldness was now sufficient to the task.

When the day of Pentecost came the disciples probably went to the Temple. This would have been proper. Some believe they remained in the Upper Room, where they had kept the Passover, but because of the large crowds involved in the moment of the coming of the Spirit, we believe that they must have been in the Temple.

The Spirit of God came upon them as they gathered in prayer, probably on Solomon's Portico in the massive Temple esplanade. There was "a rushing mighty wind" and tongues of fire that settled on the believers. The onlooking crowd was galvanized by the remarkable happenings and listened closely as Peter gave his unforgettable explanation (Acts 2:14–21).

He was eloquent, this one who had seven weeks before denied that he even knew the Lord Jesus Christ. He was utterly expert in the Scriptures, citing appropriate passages from obscure sections of the Book of Joel and the Psalms to explain the miracles. His sermon is a model of brevity and force. He spoke five minutes and three thousand people were saved.

He confronted a difficult audience, suspicious of the provincial Galileans (Acts 2:7), and secure in their knowledge of Scripture. These were the pilgrims, after all, who had made the arduous journey to Jerusalem from many a foreign land, and they were therefore serious in their relationship to God. Obviously the arrival of the Holy Spirit was timed most beneficially so that the Gospel could reach a maximum number of people. When these newly-saved ones returned to their various lands they would be full of the news of what they had seen and heard at the Temple.

The miracle of communication that occurred—that all the people understood what the disciples were saying in their own native languages—seemed to represent a directive from God that the Gospel was to be communicated in all of those lands. All present were Jews and they could have heard the message in Hebrew, but instead, no less than sixteen languages were specified in the record in which the gospel was transmitted.

Peter's argument, brilliantly reasoned from the Scriptures, deeply impressed the huge gathering. He told the crowd that they were seeing the outpouring of the Spirit of God prophesied by Joel so many centuries before (Joel 2:28) as a sign to Israel that the Messianic Age had dawned. He then reviewed the life, message, death, and resurrection of Jesus. On the resurrection, he cited King David's subtle prophecy:

For thou wilt not leave my soul in hell;
neither wilt thou suffer thine Holy One
to see corruption (Psalms 16:10).

We can imagine Peter standing there on Mount Moriah gesturing to the neighboring Mount Zion, where the mighty David lay entombed. David was not writing about himself, Peter taught, because his tomb is there to be seen. Rather, he was speaking of the Messiah. The Holy One would die, his soul would be in Sheol (the abode of the dead) but his body would not decay. Instead, the soul of the Holy One would be reunited with His body almost immediately, and Peter declared as an eye witness that this is precisely what happened to Jesus Christ. In three days He had risen from the dead just as His ancestor David had predicted.

Three thousand Israelites were utterly convinced by the rustic fishermen and made professions of faith on the spot. They were baptized at once, and the Church was born. God did not choose the number haphazardly; on the day that the law came down from Mount Sinai three thousand perished (Exodus 32:28). Indeed "the letter kills, but the Spirit gives life."

Persecution

The gospel now saturated Jerusalem as many Jewish people came to believe that Jesus was indeed their promised Messiah. But the same Sanhedrin that considered Jesus a blasphemer resolutely held their original position. They commanded Peter and John not to preach in the name of

Jesus, and when those two persisted they were punished and imprisoned.

The conflict escalated until the faithful Stephen, reckless in his defense of the Gospel, was stoned to death while preaching Christ in Jerusalem. A young Pharisee named Saul officiated at the execution, which implied that he was a member of the Sanhedrin. This is the first mention of the dynamic apostle known later as Paul; his initial appearance in scripture is as the church's sworn persecutor.

As the coercion increased in Jerusalem the believers departed and went to various cities throughout Israel, testifying of Christ as they traveled. The Word even was brought to Samaria, regarded as spiritually inferior because of its uncertain lineage. But Peter personally confirmed that the Samaritans were receiving Christ and being filled with the Spirit of God just as the full-blooded Jews were everywhere else in the land.

The Gospel did not leap from Pentecost to the Gentile cities of the world overnight. The mission to Israel itself was a complicated and necessary one as God laid the solid foundation for the later efforts of the traveling apostles. The mission to Samaria might have been thought suspect at the time, but of course the Lord Himself had graced the area with His own presence (John 4).

Gentile Salvation?

The first mission to the Gentiles was almost too much for the church to bear. The Samaritans were one thing; they were considered half-Jews. But the Gentiles were something else again.

Nevertheless, the indefatigable Peter traveled to Caesarea and witnessed there to a rather unusual Roman officer named Cornelius. Peter was reluctant about this undertaking. As a Jew he had always been under the Mosaic Law, which strictly separated the Chosen People from the Gentile ways, foods and homes, and he likely had an understandable fear of the Roman people and army that had occupied Israel for a century.

But it was definitely God's call that Peter should make this special effort. The Spirit of God had worked in both Peter and Cornelius to bring the unprecedented and world-shaking meeting together. Since the moment that Cornelius and his household believed in Jesus Christ, the world has never been the same.

Cornelius was far from the average Roman commander. He had come to believe in the God of Israel, gave generously to the poor, and was a man of prayer. He was most sensitive to spiritual promptings and he experienced a visitation from an angel to the effect that he should invite Peter to his home. Aware of the unusual circumstance, Cornelius still went ahead and sent some servants to Joppa, where they extended the invitation to the now widely known and respected apostle.

At the same time, Peter experienced a vision in which God clearly told him to eat food regarded in the Mosaic Law as unclean. Peter actually declined in the dream, but the Lord explained that He had now cleansed what was previously unacceptable. The moment he awoke, Cornelius' servants were at the door, and Peter began to realize the enormity of the coincidence. God was now going to cleanse the Gentiles as He had been cleansing the Jews, and Peter was being called upon to do the impossible.

The drama is recorded in Acts 10, in which Peter comes to the full knowledge that "God is no respecter of persons".

The Jewish believers who accompanied Peter could hardly believe their eyes as they witnessed the salvation of the first Gentiles:

> And they of the circumcision which
> believed were astonished, as many
> as came with Peter, because that on
> the Gentiles also was poured out
> the gift of the Holy Ghost (Acts 10:45).

But it was clear that Jesus Christ was received in that household as emphatically as among the Jewish believers at Pentecost. Thus, some years after the ascension of Christ, Gentile believers were admitted to the fellowship of salvation along with the Jews.

There is evidence in the record of some discomfort in Judea concerning the Gentile conversions (Acts 11:1–3). It was necessary for Peter to explain himself in Jerusalem, though, of course, that church was deeply indebted to the apostle for his previous mighty works. At length the gathered Jewish believers concluded that, strange as it seemed, Peter had indeed done the will of God:

> When they heard these things, they held
> their peace, and glorified God, saying,
> Then hath God also to the Gentiles granted
> repentance unto life (Acts 11:18).

"Saul, Why Do You Persecute Me?"

Once the Gospel was begun among the Gentiles God called forth a most unexpected personality to specialize in this difficult mission. God's ways are not our ways; which of us would have chosen Peter to speak at Pentecost, in view of his earlier disloyalty? And which of us would have selected the dangerous Saul of Tarsus for a church mission?

Paul is one of the most intriguing personalities of the Bible. He was born Saul of Tarsus in Asia Minor, studied under the leading rabbis in Jerusalem, and rose to importance among the strict religious sect of the Pharisees. He was a paragon of all that Judaism represented—he was incisively intelligent, highly educated, devout, and a conscientous follower of God and Moses. He was considered a "Pharisee of the Pharisees." The depth and breadth of his later writings confirm the heart of a complex, single-minded visionary of the faith.

But at the beginning it was this same zealousness that brought him into conflict with the fledgling church in Jerusalem. What he knew of God and the law made the worship of Jesus Christ blasphemous to him, contrary to true monotheism and a thing to be annihilated. Imprisonment and execution were the just deserts for the misguided believers in the gentle carpenter of Galilee, in Saul's view, and he surely lost little sleep over the martyrdom of Stephen.

Saul was the foremost leader of the war on Jewish Christians. His revulsion for the Jewish believers took him to distant places, wherever the preaching of Jesus had spread. On a day he was never to forget, Saul set out for Damascus armed with warrants for the arrest of the Jewish Christians there, issued by the Jerusalem Sanhedrin.

Paul met his Enemy face to face on the Damascus road as Jesus Christ Himself appeared to the persecutor in a stunning vision. The Lord rebuked him and directed him to become His servant; to represent Him to Israel and to the Gentiles!

A stumbling, blinded Paul made his way into Damascus, in no uncertain terms a believer in Jesus Christ. Recovered from his shock, he was received cautiously by the church in Damascus, who at one time would have scattered at merely the knowledge of his pending arrival. He began the hard ministry of teaching about Christ in the synagogues, and, for the first of many times, was chased out of town. The zealous Jewish religionists of the synagogues must have been dumbfounded at the change in their champion and discarded the formerly vehement one as now useless to their purposes.

A man of massive mental powers, Paul now took some time to react to it all. During the next three years we find him in obscurity in the Arabian desert. He uses this time to contemplate the radical change in his own life and the many ramifications of the Gospel of Jesus Christ. His later epistles reflect the intensity of thought and spiritual revelation that he underwent during his wilderness seclusion. He presents a picture somewhat like Moses, who repaired forty years to the desert before God called him to return to Egypt and assist in the liberation of his people.

After the sojourn, Paul returned to Damascus and then on to Jersualem, where he found agreement with the apostles. He continued on home to Tarsus, and it was there that Barnabas found him and urged him to come to Antioch to help build the new church fellowship there.

The Missionary Church

Antioch, in Syria, was rapidly replacing Jersualem as the dynamic center of the work of foreign missions. The fellowship was composed of Jewish and Gentile Christians who were energetically proclaiming Jesus Christ throughout the area. Peter, Paul, Barnabas, and several others were actively engaged in teaching the Word as the young missionaries prepared themselves for the serious and dangerous work of spreading the Gospel throughout the Empire.

Missionary activity out of Jerusalem was largely caused by the local persecution. The believers had simply run for their lives, but in running had testified to all who would listen. In Antioch, however, the climate was more accommodating and the Christians made determined plans to spread the Gospel in an orderly way. They commissioned Paul and Barnabas to be missionaries for Christ.

Paul's Initial Journey

Paul made three arduous missionary trips, preaching in the synagogues and adeptly discussing philosophy with educated Gentiles. His fourth trip, to Rome as a prisoner, is also chronicled in the Book of Acts.

The first trip was limited to the island of Cyprus and Asia Minor, in the territory we know today as Turkey. He sailed from Syria with Barnabas and Mark, and after a rewarding experience in Cyprus, went on to Asia Minor. It was then that Mark left them, much to Paul's disapproval. Nevertheless he pressed on.

Asia Minor was quite different from what Turkey is today. Those who visit southern Turkey now are repelled by the backward Moslem villages with their disheveled appearance and poor sanitation. But in the days when Paul traveled those areas numerous cities flourished, replete in their Greek culture, with temples, marketplaces and synagogues. It was to people of some sophistication that Paul brought his unique message, but he often paid the price of the radical who refuses to flinch when his convictions are challenged.

The Gospel in the Synagogue

The biblical record covers in some detail Paul's entrance into Antioch in Pisidia, an inland city of Asia Minor. Paul and Barnabas attended synagogue on the Sabbath and heard the reading of the Law and the Prophets. Then Paul, as a visiting Pharisaic Rabbi, was invited to speak.

The message he brought in Antioch is the first of three major messages of Paul recorded in Acts. It was designed to appeal particularly to the hearts and minds of his Jewish audience. He reviewed the magnificent history and traditions of Israel from the time of Moses through David to Christ. He emphasized that Jesus, the promised son of David, had died to provide forgiveness of sins, and had been raised from the dead as the prophets foretold. The content is not unlike Peter's messages to the Jewish people in Jerusalem (Acts 2–3).

This revolutionary teaching had quite an impact on the outlying synagogue. The people were polarized by Paul's view of things. The synagogue was composed of both Jews and Gentiles, since many Gentiles in the Greek-speaking countries had converted to Judaism. These sincere ones rejected the paganism and multiplicity of gods of the Greek world. They preferred, as Cornelius before them, to worship the One Creator God and to await the Messiah. They were particularly responsive to the universal message of the Gospel.

A group of Jews and Gentiles within the synagogue believed Paul's message and became the nucleus of the church in Antioch. But another group of Jews and Gentiles rejected the teaching and reacted vigorously. As happened repeatedly in Paul's missionary experience, the traditional Jewish believers in the Law sought the help of the unbelieving Gentiles to run Paul out of town (Acts 13:50).

Pursued from Antioch, Paul and Barnabas fled to Lystra and Derbe, smaller towns in the interior highlands. Paul was overtaken by the mob, stoned and left for dead. He recovered from the ordeal, however, and continued his travels. He visited a number of other towns in the area, providing both salvation and consternation to the local residents.

Finally Paul and his companions returned to the other Antioch, Syria, to report on the results of this first missionary foray. The church was genuinely pleased that the Lord had brought forth such plentiful fruit among the Gentiles of Asia Minor.

Can Gentiles Be Christians?

But there was a reaction among some of the Jewish believers in the churches of Antioch and Jerusalem about accepting Gentiles into the fellowship. They were not opposed to Gentile evangelism in principle, but they felt that those who received Christ should be circumcised and begin to keep the Law of Moses. Jesus was the *Jewish* Messiah, after all; how could those with no knowledge of Judaism walk in His footsteps?

The discussion escalated into a council, held in Jerusalem, which met to settle the matter by seeking God's will. The two sides presented their views under the leadership of James, the apostle, and he finally expressed the conviction that God did not want to impose restrictions on Gentiles— they were saved by faith in Christ alone and there were no further legal requirements. This decision of course gave further impetus to Paul's missionary work and he prepared to make a second trip, armed with the confirmation that salvation was free for the asking to everyone.

The Mission to Europe

Paul's second missionary journey was more extensive than the first. It began with a quarrel over just who would go where. Barnabas wished to accompany Paul and to take Mark again, but Paul refused to take Mark because of his previous desertion, a decision he later regretted. Thus Paul and another faithful friend, Silas, went into Asia Minor while Barnabas and Mark went elsewhere. In this manner the gospel was spread further by the vehicle of human disagreement, not an uncommon occurence during the history of the church.

Paul and Silas covered some of the same ground as in the first trip, visiting the previously established churches and confirming them in their new faith. They wanted to continue spreading the Gospel in Asia Minor where they had planted so many churches. But when they reached ancient Troy, made immortal in the writings of Homer, God led them in a totally new direction. (Acts 16:6-7). Just at that time Paul experienced a vision of a Macedonian man asking for help, and so they headed west instead for Macedonia and Greece. Obviously, this small moment of indecision and guidance from the Lord radically changed the course of history.

Paul's first European convert was a businesswoman named Lydia, a distributor of chemical dyes in the town of Philippi (Acts 16:15). At Philippi Paul had again the experience that was now becoming typical for him; many received Christ, but Paul and Silas were jailed for their efforts. Through a series of miraculous events they were released, and their jailer became a believer and was baptized!

From Philippi they went on to Thessalonica where there was enough of a Jewish population to justify a synagogue. For three Saturdays Paul told the congregation of the Good News. He was able to teach about Christ, entirely out of the Old Testament of course, as few of us are today. As happened previously in Asia Minor, some Jews and Gentiles believed and some did not. The unbelieving contingents gave Paul his usual invitation to leave (they kicked him out of town), but the new church survived and prospered. It was becoming a repetitive cycle of negative experiences, but through this methodology Paul was able to establish churches in a few weeks' time.

Athens and Corinth

Now Paul took on some big cities. He might have been faulted to this point for sticking to quiet villages and small towns, and generally addressing the less aware. But at Athens, the hub of learning and culture of the Greek-speaking world, the energetic missionary confronted the most worldly and skeptical of intellectuals.

He testified in the many synagogues and business areas for a time, and eventually was invited to make his presentation to the remarkable forum of ideas known as Mars Hill. The Acropolis, with the magnificent Parthenon, stood just adjacent and in view of the assembled intelligentsia, who enjoyed debating at length the nature of man, the universe, and whatever god or gods an interesting visitor might care to proffr.

In excellent Greek Paul addressed the philosophically learned multitude. The message is faithfully recorded in Acts as Paul's second major address in that book. He departed somewhat from his earlier sermons before the Jews in that he now had idol worshippers to deal with.

Their many gods, he told them, were no substitute for the one true God Who had created the universe. At issue was nothing less than life and death. God had sent Someone who would judge the world and who had risen from the dead. All will rise who believe in Him.

If Paul had met informed opposition from the Jews, he now met with derisive indifference from the Gentiles. The self-styled enlightened ones laughed him to scorn when he preached the resurrection of Christ. All the same, some wanted to hear more, and some Athenians came to salvation during Paul's ministry there (Acts 17:22–32).

From the sublime surroundings of Athens Paul moved on to the bustling commercial port of Corinth. It was the sin capital of Greece, the Apostle well knew, but when had Jesus Christ avoided sinners?

Indeed Paul found more acceptance among the Jews and Gentiles of teeming Corinth than he had enjoyed at Athens; he spent eighteen months there leading sundry souls to the Lord and teaching them the Word of God. A Hebrew Christian couple named Aquilla and Priscilla assisted him in Corinth. The three of them worked together, supporting themselves through the trade of tent-making, and firmly planted an important Christian Church.

Finally Paul returned, deeply satisfied, to Jerusalem and then to Antioch in Syria with a glowing missionary report. There had been much opposition but the Gospel had been spread widely and new churches had been established throughout Asia Minor and in Greece.

The Ministry at Ephesus

Paul took some time off in Antioch, refreshing himself in the fellowship of his home church before setting out for his third and final missionary journey as reported in Acts. He was not to travel as a free man again.

He began with the original areas in Asia Minor, encouraging the brethren in the cities and towns where he had previously started churches. But when he arrived at Ephesus he found a marvelous acceptance and a ministry that was to last almost three years. His friends Aquilla and Priscilla, and one of their talented converts, Apollos, had already done effective groundwork in that beautiful and historic city.

When Paul arrived he was warmly welcomed. He spent three months in the synagogue sharing the Gospel of Christ "boldly" (Acts 19:8–9). Eventually his preaching had the by now familiar effect of sharply dividing his listeners, and the ever doubting Jewish worshippers began to speak against Paul and his novel ideas.

This time, however, there was a true force of believers, Jews and Gentiles, and Paul separated them from the synagogue and took them to the already existing lecture hall of Tyrannus. There he conducted something of a one-man seminary, teaching daily for some two years. The results of this ministry were truly amazing:

And this continued by the space of
two years; so that all they which
dwelt in Asia heard the word of the
Lord Jesus, both Jews and Greeks
(Acts 19:10).

Paul's ministry was vindicated in an interesting way when a Jewish priest named Sceva, who practiced exorcism, tried to cast out a demon in the name of Jesus. This imitation of a good thing backfired, however, and when the demon spoke Sceva was terrified. The demon said he knew Jesus and Paul but was not acquainted with Sceva, and the demon assaulted the priest! As a result many Jews and Gentiles received Christ and deserted the sorcery that had become popular in Ephesus.

As a matter of fact, so many pagans received Christ that the matter came to the attention of the local idol makers. The new converts certainly had no use for the silver idols which had been big business in Ephesus before Paul's arrival. Demetrius, the head of the silversmith's guild, called a general meeting, declaring that their very industry was in danger of collapse and that even the temple of Diana, the reigning goddess, was threatened. The entire city was drawn into turmoil at the 24,000-seat amphitheater, and finally the mayor appealed to the citizens to hold their peace. General unrest had a way of attracting the murderous attention of Rome. The mayor pleaded with the crowd to disperse and at length he was successful.

After this uproar Paul felt his ministry in Ephesus had been completed. A handful of Christians had overturned a populous city. Paul continued on to Macedonia and Greece, exhorting the churches he had established there on his previous trip. He then began to make plans for a fateful and difficult return to Jerusalem.

A Dangerous Journey

For some time Paul had been concerned about the "poor saints in Jerusalem." He had written to churches and received offerings on their behalf since they were not only enduring persecution but also a long-standing famine (Acts 20:20–23). Paul wanted to return to Jerusalem with the funds from the Gentile churches, and he also felt led to be in the Holy City for the Feast of Pentecost.

But even as he began his trip there was a sense of foreboding. Jewish Christians were not well liked in Jerusalem, the city of the Temple of God, and Paul's reputation as a key evangelist had preceded him. The rabbi from Antioch was a marked man. Realizing that the possibility of an early death awaited him in the Holy City he took the opportunity, when his ship docked near Ephesus, to call for the elders of the church to meet him at the harbor. There he delivered his third major message recorded in Acts. Thus we see that the three parts of humanity are covered in the three messages: the Jews first, in the synagogues Paul visited; the Gentiles, in the cities of the Empire; and now the Church.

It was an emotional occasion at the Ephesian docks as

the dedicated elders met with their mentor in the faith. Paul encouraged them to continue in their ministry for Christ and warned them that false teachers would come in to disrupt the Church. The elders were most concerned that this might be the last time they would see Paul. They embraced him as he embarked, with many a prayer for his fateful journey to Jerusalem.

As Paul continued on he was warned several times to avoid Jerusalem because of the difficult situation there, but he persisted (Acts 21:13–14). Some suppose that Paul was acting in disobedience to God by insisting on an ill-advised mission. But a broader view of Paul's ultimate ministry indicates that the trip was all part of the Lord's plan to bring the Gospel to Rome. The repeated warnings in the record merely stress the hazards and the spiritual courage required of those who would answer the missionary calling. Paul was later to write to the Romans:

And we know that all things work
together for good to them that love
God, to them who are the called
according to his purpose (Romans 8:28).

Paul was now accompanied by a Gentile Christian of Ephesus named Trophimus, who was to testify to the church at Jerusalem. Trophimus would serve as an example of encouragement to the beleaguered Jewish Christians of Israel—that Gentiles were coming to the Jewish Messiah throughout the Empire.

At Jerusalem Paul informed the church of all that the Lord had done in establishing churches among the Gentile nations, and his audience expressed much appreciation for his hard ministry (Acts 21:27–29). But when he went to the Temple he was arrested. The outraged Jewish worshipers mistakenly thought he had desecrated the holy site by bringing a Gentile there. Trophimus was the problem, but such was the zeal of the Temple worshipers to apprehend Paul that they overlooked the fact that the Ephesian never entered the Temple (Acts 21:29).

The crowd dragged Paul out of the Temple enclosure into the Court of the Gentiles and shut the gates of the Temple building (Acts 21:30). They turned him over to a Roman officer who was to take him into the neighboring Tower of Antonia for imprisonment. But Paul asked the officer if he could address the crowd. He then related his testimony of how he had received Christ and become a missionary to the Gentiles, but the Israelites were infuriated. The dramatic scene came to a head with Paul's incarceration.

The remaining eight chapters of Acts, almost one-third of the book, tell in high detail of Paul's arrest in Jerusalem, his trials before Festus and Agrippa in Caesarea, his appeal to Caesar, and his harrowing voyage to Rome. If the Empire thought they would interfere with Paul's mission by taking him to the capital they were wrong. Ultimately Paul was able to promulgate the Gospel effectively in Rome, even as a prisoner.

The Book of Acts concludes with Paul's two-year house arrest in Rome while awaiting his appearance before Caesar.

5

The New Message
(Romans, Galatians,
Thessalonians, Colossians,
Philippians, and Philemon)

The new people of God understood the basics of the message of salvation through Christ. Those whom God called out, known as the Church, had begun a pilgrimage in the earth which is still going on. The Church is not truly "at home" in this world but must sojourn here until the return of the Lord. This is problematical.

We must appreciate that they had no New Testament, at first, through which to comprehend the new message. The Lord had promised that the indwelling Holy Spirit would guide the Apostles and the Church in all truth (John 16:13), and so the New Testament was revealed a little at a time. Shortly after the Church was formed the Apostles began writing inspired accounts of the life of Jesus Christ and instruction for the believers, in epistles, or letters.

The new believers needed to understand how the new message differed from the Law of Moses and the pagan religious philosophies they were accustomed to as Jews and Gentiles respectively. The Gospel is complex in its simplicity. Just how was it that faith in Christ provided salvation from sin, daily victory, and eternal life? It should be realized that errors and heresies sprang up in the Church almost as it began. The new people of God struggled with the false teachings of legalism, gnosticism, and various other misinterpretations. This is not entirely a thing of the past. The Church today, armed with the complete New Testament and millions of words of learned commentary on it, still wrestles with errors of fact and doctrine even as they did in the first century.

A number of the letters written by Paul to specific churches were designed primarily to explain in great detail the new message—the body of truth and revelation from the Lord Jesus Christ. In carrying on with the necessities of his missionary ministry the Apostle wrote the best-read letters in all of history.

Romans: Sin and Deliverance

Paul's copious letter to the church in Rome has been called the cathedral of the Christian faith. Its sixteen chapters detail a comprehensive systematic theology, dealing with the central themes of the faith. It was not actually the Apostle's first letter but one of his earlier ones. Its topics cover the range of human experience.

To begin with, writes the Apostle, all of humanity is condemned in sin. God has provided salvation from sin and its consequence, death, through Christ. This salvation is available to everyone through faith—the utterly trusting kind of faith that Abraham had. Once a human being possesses salvation in Christ he becomes a different order of person, not subject to legalisms such as the law of Moses, but guided directly by the indwelling Spirit of God. Victory over the persistent sin nature and the guarantee of eternal life are awarded to the indwelt believer.

All of the above is set forth in writing that presents an intriguing mixture of argumentation from the Old Testament, broad human experience, and the keen intellect of the insightful Apostle. Paul's style is compelling, even hostile readers must agree.

> For all have sinned, and come short of
> the glory of God (Romans 3:23).

With this statement, written to every human being who has ever lived, Paul establishes the universal dominance of sin. All men stand condemned before God as sinners both by practice and by inheritance. Gentiles are sinners because whatever they knew of God they cast aside in favor of worshiping idols or humanity itself. The Jews are sinners because despite the advantages and privileges of being the Chosen Nation they have never been able to keep God's excellent Law. Ironically the Law of Moses tended to show Israel her grave shortcomings rather than having the effect of bringing them to righteousness, observes Paul.

We are all sinners, not only because we all practice sin, but because we are born sinners. Our sinful nature has been inherited from our first parents, Adam and Eve (Romans 5:12). While some people may think of the story of Adam and Eve as a myth, the Bible never does. Paul asserts repeatedly that our basic problem stems from Adam's desertion from God's will. We are imprisoned in the situation of living. Our lives are cut short by the wages of sin: death. The death of an unbelieving sinner is both physical and eternal. Its momentous consequence is utter separation from God forever.

God's solution to this dilemma runs contrary to human rationality:

> But God commendeth his love toward us, in

> that, while we were yet sinners, Christ died
> for us (Romans 5:8).

Christ did not die for some supposed race of good people,
He died for a mass of indistinguishable sinners. Divine redemption and eternal life are given freely to the worst of
us.

The transmission of the Gospel is just as simple. It is
spoken by human mouths, heard by human ears, and simply believed (Romans 3:29–30; 4:3; 10:17). Faith in the
death and resurrection of Christ guarantees salvation, and
that's all there is to that. By simple faith a lost sinner is
transformed into a forgiven sinner, a child of God, an heir
of eternal life, and a new creature—one indwelt perpetually
by the Spirit of God.

A tremendous amount of philosophy has poured forth
in response to this pure and unadulterated Good News.
Human nature seems repelled by the divine logic. The elegant plan of salvation through unadorned faith is considered too easy or too difficult or too unreasonable or whatever. The human race has, by and large, rejected or
remained in ignorance of the supernatural plan.

Abraham's faith is Paul's key example. Abraham believed
that he and Sarah would have the son promised to him
even though Sarah's childbearing years had long since
passed. He believed that God would fulfill His covenant and
he implicitly believed that God would continue to do what
an ordinary man would consider the impossible. That kind
of faith in God believes He could and did raise Christ from
the dead.

Paul's exhaustive definitions and descriptions of the faith
assure the believers' victory over sin in daily life and the
confidence that no power can ever separate them from
God's love (Romans 8:38–39). It must have been a reju-
venating message for those who had in their lineage so little
knowledge of the nature of the true God. The Gentiles must

have been greatly encouraged. But Paul does not omit a special message concerning the convenant nation. He writes with vivid clarity about the condition of Israel, his home.

The nation of Israel had missed the hour of visitation (Luke 19:44), and the Church had been created as the vehicle of the Gospel. Jewish people were coming to faith in Christ in the various nations, of course, but what would become of the Chosen People and Promised Land? Had the Jews now been discarded as the Chosen People? Had an offended God now canceled His covenants and promises to them? Was the Church, inevitably to be composed of a greater and greater majority of Gentiles, now the sole repository for the divine promises made to Israel? Had the Messianic Kingdom Age been set aside or transformed into a kind of kingdom led by the new Church?

They were good questions at the time, and many Gentile Christians began to adopt those views concerning Israel. In fact, much of professing Christianity still clings to that sort of interpretation of the destiny of the Covenant People and the Holy Land—that the old covenants have been canceled and God's promises are no longer operative. But the Apostle wrote in painstaking detail to show that while the Jewish people are currently partially blind to the Gospel, God is not at all finished with those He chose:

> I say then, Hath God cast away his people?
> God forbid. For I also am an Israelite, of
> the seed of Abraham, of the tribe of
> Benjamin (Romans 11:1).

It is clear that a remnant of Jewish people have believed in Jesus Christ throughout the Church Age, including all of the apostles and many outstanding leaders in church history. Moreover, the entire nation of Israel that survives the awesome end times and war of Armaggedon will be saved at the second coming of the Messiah:

> And so all Israel shall be saved: as it is

written, There shall come out of Sion the
Deliverer, and shall turn away ungodliness
from Jacob (Romans 11:26).

Obviously the Messianic Age promised to Israel has not
been canceled but merely postponed. In the meanwhile,
God is fulfilling His plans for the Church Age and then He
will prepare Israel for the return of her King. When Christ
comes back to Israel the nation will receive Him gladly and
then enter into the fulness of her convenant relationship
with God.

After settling the important question of Israel and God's
promises, Paul devotes the final five chapters of this con-
summate epistle to practical Christian living. He writes of
consecration and service, and, most profoundly, about human relations. In light of all the truths revealed about salvation, victory, and the relationship of the Church to God
and to Israel, Paul exhorts the Roman Christians to dedicate
themselves completely to God and to walk in the power of
His Spirit. Love is the theme, inevitably, in Paul's instructions on how the Church and the Christian individual should
live day by day.

Grace and the Galatians

The Galatians seemed not to realize the full impact of
grace, especially when it concerned the Gentiles. Most of
the Jewish Christians were happy to welcome the new Gentile believers freely into the congregations throughout the
Empire with no special requirements. But some of the Jewish charter members were energetically opposed to this practice. They felt that Gentile believers would need to become
Jews if they were to be true Christians (Galatians 6:12–13).
Conversion to Judaism would involve the rites of circum-

cision, the dietary regulations, and the other stipulations of the Law of Moses. If they didn't do these things, the Gentile followers of Christ really couldn't be admitted to the full fellowship of the Church, they felt.

Paul reacted with indignation when he heard that this teaching was rampant in the Galatian area of Asia Minor, where he had established many churches. His letter to the Galatians brims with righteous anger, brilliant defenses of the true faith, and beseeching exhortations. Paul saw this teaching, about which he had debated in Jerusalem, as a threat to the unity of the Church and even an undermining of salvation by grace. The Galatians were adding to the Gospel, he said. He went to great pains to demonstrate that he was a genuine apostle of Christ, that his doctrine had been approved by the Church of Jerusalem, and that the Old Testament verifies that true salvation comes only by God's promise and not by human effort. The teachings of the circumcision sect were anathema to genuine Christianity and the pure gospel of Christ, he stated in the most emphatic terms.

An interesting Old Testament parallel that Paul used to buttress his argument was that of Abraham's family. Isaac was Abraham's seed of promise through his wife Sarah, while Ishmael was his son through his servant Hagar and human contrivance. Scripture declared most plainly that Ishmael would not inherit the divine promise with Isaac:

Nevertheless what saith the scripture?
Cast out the bondwoman and her son: for
the son of the bondwoman shall not be
heir with the son of the freewoman.

So then, brethren, we are not children
of the bondwoman, but of the free
(Galatians 4:30–31).

Thus the true inheritors of God's blessing today are those

who believe in God's promises about His Son. Those who claim mere physical descendency from Abraham do not inherit the blessing.

The Second Coming and the Thessalonians

The church at Thessalonica was basically sound and thriving, but they were disturbed about Christ's Second Coming. Paul wrote two letters that helped clarify this technical point in the new message.

They certainly believed in the Lord's imminent return, about which they had been taught very completely. They realized they would be caught up, in what is known as the Rapture, to meet Christ in the air. But some of their brothers and sisters in Christ had died and they were concerned that those might miss the glory of this resurrection. Paul reassured them that the ones who had died would surely not miss the Rapture. On the contrary, they would have a very prominent place in that event:

> For the Lord himself shall descend from
> heaven with a shout, with the voice of the
> archangel, and with the trump of God:
> and the dead in Christ shall rise first.

> Then we which are alive and remain shall
> be caught up together with them in the
> clouds, to meet the Lord in the air: and
> so shall we ever be with the Lord
> (1 Thessalonians 4:16–7).

Then, later on, the Thessalonians had other questions about prophecy. Someone had been spreading the word that the Day of the Lord had already come. Had they missed the Rapture? Were they going to have to endure the dreaded tribulation time of judgment on the world?

Paul comforted them greatly in his second letter, which stated that the Day of the Lord could not occur until certain easily identified events had transpired. The events included a "falling away" (which may mean moral apostasy, but may also mean the departure of the church in the Rapture), and the removal of the One who restrains evil (the Holy Spirit), and the emergence of the Man of Sin, the Antichrist. Until those clarion issues of prophecy take place the Day of the Lord's judgment will not commence (2 Thessalonians 2:1–9).

We wait even today, in fact, for these prophetic events to take place. We still await the Rapture of the Church and the time when the world will yet face the Day of the Lord.

The Colossians and the Gnostics

Just as the Jewish Christians had their heretical tendencies, so did the Gentile Christians. Legalism, the Law of Moses, and circumcision were not the Gentiles' stumbling block, of course, but they managed to get caught up in a spiritistic philosophy called Gnosticism.

Gnosticism means "knowledge" and was a combination of the idea of secret knowledge held only by a select body of initiates, that there was a gradation of supernatural beings ranging from various grades of angels, to Christ, to God. They did not believe in the Deity of Christ but viewed Him rather as a kind of super angel. Derivations of this sort of heresy are rampant today in various cults and certain liberal elements of professing Christianity.

The Colossians were confused by this distorted doctrine, and Paul's letter to them stressed that they should not seek

after such peculiar worldly diversions. They should instead
realize that the Lord Jesus Christ, Himself certainly Deity,
is the repository of all spiritual wisdom:

> That their hearts might be comforted, being
> knit together in love, and unto all riches
> of the full assurance of understanding, to
> the acknowledgement of the mystery of God,
> and of the Father, and of Christ;
>
> In whom are hid all the treasures of wisdom
> and knowledge (Colossians 2:2–3).

Much later, toward the close of the Apostolic century, the
Apostle John had to struggle with Gnosticism again. The
doctrine had spread and intensified. By that time Gnostics
were teaching that not only was Christ not God, but He was
also not fully human. John declared this teaching as tan-
tamount to denying the faith:

> Hereby know ye the Spirit of God: Every
> spirit that confesseth that Jesus Christ
> is come in the flesh is of God:
>
> And every spirit that confesseth not that
> Jesus Christ is come in the flesh is not
> of God: and this is that spirit of anti-
> christ, whereof ye have heard that it
> should come; and even now already is it
> in the world (1 John 4:2–3).

In each of John's three letters he took vigorous issue with
the Gnostic heresy and its teachers, warning the churches
against their devastating effects.

Greetings to the Philippians and Philemon

The Philippians received a pleasant letter from Paul, who
was in the direst of circumstances when he wrote it. His

focus this time was not one of correcting a doctrinal or practical error but rather to express his appreciation for their support, prayer, and encouragement. Imprisoned in Rome and awaiting Caesar's judgment, the Apostle exhorts the Philippians to continue in their faithfulness.

Fully realizing that death might be imminent for him, Paul wrestled with whether he would rather stay in this life or die and go to the Lord. This must have been a most instructive part of the new message. The Christian does not fear death, and Paul's conclusion was that it would be better for him personally to die. If, however, it would be better for the churches for Paul to remain on earth, he was surely willing to do so (Philippians 1:21–26). In his dark cell Paul is able to discuss matter of factly his own death and the improvement it will provide him. He also exalted over the very joy of life in Christ.

Another of the letters that emphasized the new message was the brief note from Paul to Philemon, a leader of the Church in Colosse. Philemon's slave, Onesimus, had run away to Rome, stumbled on to Paul, and received the Lord. Paul asked Philemon to receive his runaway slave as a brother in Christ and not to punish him. The letter is a touching example of how transforming is the new message. The gospel dramatically affects social and legal customs, then and now.

Contend for the Faith

Thus it is that in the various letters inspired by the Spirit and written by the Apostles, the new message of the crucified and risen Messiah is developed against the crucible of conflict and human experience. It was one thing to believe in Christ, quite another to confront life in this world while holding such a belief.

The epistles explaining the doctrine and practice of Christianity remain a uniquely useful body of writing. Jude sums it up in his single chapter:

> Beloved, when I gave all diligence to
> write unto you of the common salvation,
> it was needful for me to write unto
> you, and exhort you that ye should
> earnestly contend for the faith which
> was once delivered unto the saints
> (Jude 3).

6

The New People
(Ephesians, Corinthians)

The Church was off and running before anyone knew what it was. The new people had no prior experience with which to compare their new circumstances.

Moses never went to church and never knew there would even be a church. The apostles themselves knew almost nothing about the church until the Holy Spirit came to start forming it. Only after the infant church began to grow and spread did its leaders begin to grasp the revolutionary nature of their calling.

Peter must have been taken aback as he saw the ministry develop from a group of three thousand people, who happened to be on hand for a propitious miracle, to an organization spread all over the Empire. He faithfully reported the amazing spreading of the Gospel, from Judea to Samaria to Galilee and then across the seas, at the various councils of the leaders of the new faith.

But it was to Paul that the Lord gave the most comprehensive and clearest revelations about the nature, purpose, destiny, and conduct of the new people. His letters to the Ephesian and Corinthian congregations were particularly concerned with these issues.

The Universal Church

The church is addressed as both universal—the collective body of believers in Jesus Christ—and local—the believers of some given congregation. The letter to the Ephesians takes up the concept of the universal church more than any other part of the New Testament.

God is creating a new people—different from Israel, different from the Gentile nations. They are the "called out" ones, called out of the culture of the world and placed in a new culture that is distinctive in every aspect. The new people are called out from both Jewish and Gentile communities, their human origins, and placed into one new entity, the Church. We are seated together in heavenly places in Christ Jesus (Ephesians 2:6).

The church is referred to as the "body of Christ." The universal church is a kind of spiritual body with Christ as the head and the numerous individuals in the church as the various parts of the body. The Head directs the affairs of His body and is the "fulness of him that filleth all in all" (Ephesians 1:22–23).

The church is also described as the "bride of Christ." The Lord is seen as the husband while the church is the bride that will be presented to Him ultimately at His return. One of the "mysteries" (truths previously hidden but now revealed) was the oneness of the church and Christ, as with the first husband and wife, Adam and Eve (Ephesians 5:25–32).

This is one of the tenderest and most appealing analogies in all Scripture. Christ is the leader, comforter, and savior of His bride; the church is the chaste, beautiful, obedient, loving bride of the Lord. Millions of wedding ceremonies have been conducted with the words of Paul in Ephesians

5 concerning the touching image of Christ and His Church as the ultimate wedded couple.

The Local Church

The epistles contain far more material about the local church. The universal church is described only occasionally, but the local church is addressed and alluded to hundreds of times throughout the New Testament. The local church is the earthly touchstone of all the epistles, and its hopes and dreams, as well as its myriad problems, are approached frankly and decisively. The new people were handled with care as only God can care.

As in the case of the universal church the local church is seen as a body of Christ. But the members are featured in their various practical functions, use of gifts, and inter-relationships. The organization of the local church is really the outworking of the universal church concept on the local level. To a large extent the organization followed closely that of the Jewish synagogue.

Despite the unvarnished message of the New Testament epistles, church members today tend to think of the first century church as paragons of the faith. But if we take the Scriptures at face value we find that there were some serious problems. There were false brethren in the local churches, people who professed to have received Christ but had not really done so. Those who had genuinely come to know the Lord had brought with them into the local church some of their old natures, that much is clear. There was a very real internal conflict within each believer and also a certain amount of strife among the groups as a whole. All sorts of doctrinal and practical problems developed in the early church and, truth to tell, most of them are still with us.

Corinth is a pristine example of the problematical local

church. The "Sodom and Gommorah" atmosphere of that sinful city may well have made some of its inhabitants more receptive to the gospel of grace and forgiveness. But it also exposed them to moral and organizational problems that required apostolic correction.

In his first letter to the Corinthians Paul uses divinely inspired logic to deal with the problems of divisiveness, difficulties over marriage, a case of incest, abuses of the Lord's Supper, and slothfulness in the Lord's work. He also discusses the appropriate use of the various spiritual gifts.

Who Died for You?

Denominationalism seemed to have had its origins in Corinth. The believers were beginning to cluster around various leaders and to compete over just which group had the superior doctrine and teaching. Some looked to Paul and his acclaimed accomplishments, while others felt that Peter was the one to follow since he had been among the original twelve disciples. Still others felt that the message of the industrious Old Testament expert, Apollos, was superior. Apollos, a Hebrew Christian scholar from the university community of Alexandria, Egypt, held his audiences spellbound with his discussion on Christ as the fulfillment of Messianic prophecy. The church was certainly divided in doctrine and in its operations, and Paul was distressed:

> For it hath been declared unto me of you, my brethren, by them which are of the house of Chloe, that there are contentions among you.

> Now this I say, that every one of you saith, I am of Paul; and I of Apollos; and I of Cephas; and I of Christ.

Is Christ divided? was Paul crucified
for you? or were ye baptized in the
name of Paul? (1 Corinthians 1:11–13).

The Apostle pointed the church to the Lord. While God
had given the church various teachers and leaders with
various functions and responsibilities, none certainly could
take precedence over the Lord Jesus Himself. He is the One
Who was crucified for us. He is the One Who gives us
eternal life. He is the Head of our Church (1 Corinthians
1:13,30).

In our dealings with other believers, Christ must be
preeminent and all earthly leaders and issues secondary. In
true Christianity there is no hierarchy of people. We are all
sinners level at the cross. Various ones are called forth who
possess various gifts, and they may exercise those gifts in
positions of leadership. But it becomes simply another kind
of humanism for the Christian church to look to a man for
guidance rather than to the Lord.

The problem hasn't gotten any easier since Corinth. One
of the greater struggles Christians have had throughout the
centuries is maintaining a proper relationship with other
believers while at the same time holding fast to the closest
possible relationship with Jesus Christ.

Should I Marry?

Naturally, some of the believers in Corinth wanted to
marry but they were not certain how their plans fit into the
Lord's design for the church. Considering the atmosphere
of persecution and the anticipated return of the Lord, the
question of marriage was worthy of inquiry to Paul.

His instruction on the matter drew attention to the turmoils of the times and the precarious position of some Christians. Already there had been many believers imprisoned, and even martyred, for their faith. The Gospel was coming into violent conflict with both Old Covenant Judaism and Roman paganism. In view of the situation Paul urged the young believers to think twice about entering into marriage. However, he said, he didn't want to put an undue burden on them, and he indicated that it certainly was acceptable for them to marry, as long as they fully understood the difficulties of their position (1 Corinthians 7:2,8,10,26).

Freedom or License?

A serious abuse of the liberty in Christ developed in Corinth. One of the men of the church was living with his father's estranged wife (1 Corinthians 5:1–6). The incestuous relationship was in violation of the Law of Moses, as well as Roman law, but the perpetrator openly boasted of his freedom to do such things in Christ. He indicated that he was not going to be bound by any laws, and his attitude was anything but repentant.

Paul exploded with the same fervor he gave forth in the letter to the Galatians. Those legalistic ones were guilty of "too much law," and now there was sort of a case of "too much grace." He advised the church not to tolerate the flaunting of moral precepts and that our liberty in Christ does not extend to a license for immorality. The very name of Jesus Christ was brought into disrepute among the unbelievers by such behavior, Paul pointed out. He counseled the church to rebuke the unprincipled brother, and that if he didn't change his ways, to withdraw their fellowship from him. The situation represented one of the first examples of how discipline within the church was to be handled.

The Lord's Supper and the Gifts

Christ had committed to the church the ordinance of the Lord's Supper or Communion. Communion is the reenactment of what Jesus did at the Passover feast before He died. The disciples were to take the bread and wine, perpetually, as a memorial of His body and blood given for them as the ultimate sacrifice.

The church at Corinth was practicing communion, but somehow the solemn ceremony was getting out of hand. Some families were bringing substantial meals to eat during the memorial while others did not or could not do so. Some others were actually overdoing it with the wine, getting drunk in the process of commemorating the Lord's Supper! Paul urged them to emphasize the simple beauty of the ordinance. It was hardly a time for revelry but rather a personal examination of their own lives before the Lord. Joyful eating and drinking was no sin, but this should be done at home and not while the church was memorializing the death of Jesus Christ (1 Corinthians 11:21–22).

A like problem developed in the worship services as the robust Corinthians let their feelings loose in unseemly ways. Disruption occurred as one teacher would interrupt another in the midst of his lesson. Women were trying to teach biblical doctrine to the men, a situation certainly never seen in any synagogue. People would rise and speak in a tongue no one in the audience could understand or interpret. The confusion would impress a stranger who visited the church with the idea that something was very wrong with the believers (1 Corinthians 14:23).

Paul's instruction concerned his concept of the ideal worship service. Those with the appropriate gifts of communication would address the church in some kind of reasonable order, teaching, exhorting, encouraging, and praying. The women were not to have authority over the men nor attempt to teach them doctrine; they were more susceptible to doctrinal error and deception, as Eve was deceived by Satan in the Garden of Eden (1 Timothy 2:12–14).

Also the remarkable gift of tongues, through which God gave various revelations to the infant church, was to be used most sparingly and only when a qualified interpreter was present. The Apostle reminded them that while all the believers had at least one gift, some of the gifts were permanent in the church while others were temporary signs for the early stages (1 Corinthians 13:8–10).

Furthermore all of the gifts were to be exercised harmoniously within the church, just as the various organs and members of the human body function in harmony. The guiding principle was to be "agape," a word translated as love. The concept of agape is more far-reaching than mere human love. Agape is a divinely-motivated unselfish concern and compassion toward the church and the outside world. One of the best loved portions of the Bible is Paul's majestic portrayal of this sort of love in 1 Corinthians 13.

The Resurrection and the Life

The Corinthians also had a problem with the resurrection of the dead. Some of the church believed that there simply wouldn't be any such thing, and they ridiculed the idea that dead bodies would come up out of their graves. Others believed in the resurrection at Christ's return and used the doctrine as an excuse to sit back and do nothing; they would bide their time until the Lord came for them and then, dead or alive, they would go on to greater things.

The Apostle vigorously answered both errors. He argued that if there were no resurrection then Jesus Himself didn't rise from the dead. And if Jesus didn't rise then there was no atonement made for our sins, and we who believe in Him have a worse than useless faith. We are being persecuted now and have nothing to look forward to in the future. We are to be pitied. But Christ *did* rise, insisted Paul. He was seen by the disciples and five hundred Israelites at one time, and His resurrection provides the guarantee that our atonement is very real and that we ourselves will be resurrected (1 Corinthians 15:3–8, 20).

And what effect should this overwhelming promise have on our daily lives? Should we really just relax and await our total transformation? Absolutely not, says Paul forcefully. Such a promise should energize us to live the most productive lives possible for each of us because we are confident that everything we do for Christ will have *eternal* significance!

> Therefore, my beloved brethren, be ye
> steadfast, unmoveable, always abounding
> in the work of the Lord, forasmuch as
> ye know that your labour is not in vain
> in the Lord (1 Corinthians 15:58).

Paul's second letter to the Corinthians is an autographical piece of the most touching candor. Rather than rebuking the much flawed church for their errors, he seeks to encourage and comfort them in their difficulties. In truth, the Corinthians were suffering for their faith in Christ and they needed encouragement.

They had taken the prescribed action against the one who had committed that flagrant incest, but they refused to let him back into the fellowship of the church even though he had terminated the relationship and repented. By their lack of forgiveness they were being unchristian. And, in another more grave problem, some of the element of the church who disagreed with Paul's teachings were attacking his actual validity as a true apostle of Christ.

Putting himself last, Paul began by urging them to receive the repentant brother back into the fellowship. He then comforted them in their sufferings and defended his apostleship by reviewing his own life. Even though it was relatively early in his missionary career, Paul had suffered extensive hardships and punishments for the Gospel of Christ:

Are they ministers of Christ? (I speak
as a fool) I am more: in labours more
abundant, in stripes above measure, in
prisons more frequent, in deaths oft.

Of the Jews five times received I forty
stripes save one.

Thrice was I beaten with rods, once was
I stoned, thrice I suffered shipwreck,
a night and a day I have been in the
deep;

In journeyings often, in perils of
waters, in perils of robbers, in perils
by mine own countrymen, in perils by
the heathen, in perils in the city, in
perils in the wilderness, in perils in
the sea, in perils among false brethren;

In weariness and painfulness, in watchings
often, in hunger and thirst, in fastings
often, in cold and nakedness.

Beside those things that are without, that
which cometh upon me daily, the care of all the
churches (2 Corinthians 11:23-28).

Paul's justifications of his position and his good works should not have been necessary at all, but his deeply personal insights and his defenses of the faith inspire us. He pleaded with the Corinthian Christians to follow him, as he sought to follow the Lord, through persecution and suffering. They would all have the ultimate destiny of blessing from the Lord together.

Corinth Lives

In reading all of the above, the sincere Christian will come to the understanding that the new people are still the new people. Evidently no one has become an expert Christian, and the problems of the volatile Corinth carry on in the church to the present time. The New Testament revelation is now complete, and the Lord continues to call out new members of the body and bride of Christ. True believers in the Lord Jesus Christ are to be found almost everywhere in the world, forming local congregations that preach Christ and struggle with the daily problems of persecution and misunderstanding. The church is maligned from without and within and is still prey to divisions, disruptions, and false teachings.

For nineteen centuries this remarkable new people has existed through feast and famine, through governmental persecution and blessing, and through internal stresses of division and union. It stands firm on the Lord's promises that His "ekklesia" church will endure throughout the age, with all of its problems and blessings, until He returns to claim it for His own.

7

The New Leaders
(Timothy and Titus)

The years passed. Thousands were saved and were awaiting the imminent return of Jesus Christ. But the Lord still tarried and His apostles grew older.

It became clear after thirty years since the ascension of Christ that new leaders would be needed to carry on the apostolic work of spreading the Gospel. New areas and new generations would need the saving message. By now Paul, Peter, and even the youngest apostle, John, were getting along in years. Some of the apostles had already died and gone on to the Lord. Some had been martyred for their faith.

Obviously the church would languish if all of the apostles perished and Jesus had not yet returned. Who would lead the churches? Who would pastor the flocks? Who would teach the believers and expound the Word?

The apostles began to train new leaders from among those the Lord had called. Paul had his Timothy and Titus, Peter had his Mark, and John had a number of spiritual proteges not named in the Scriptures, but who played a prominent role in the new era. The second century A.D. would come to be known as that of the early church fathers. The second generation leaders would now emerge.

They did not and could not have the authority nor meet

the qualifications of the apostles. It was required of an apostle that he actually had seen the resurrected Christ and possessed the Lord's own commission to communicate true doctrine to the infant church. The apostles, along with Christ the cornerstone, were the historical foundation of the church. Now everything else had to be built on that sure foundation.

"My Own Son in the Faith"

Paul called the faithful Timothy his son in the faith. To him and to Titus the great apostle wrote the pastoral letters, with their intensive instructions on how to lead in the new era.

Timothy came from Lystra, one of the smaller towns in the interior of Asia Minor, not far from Paul's home town of Tarsus. Paul had led Timothy to the Lord personally during his second missionary journey and from there on took him along in his travels.

The new leader was half Jewish. His mother had raised him to love and respect the Old Testament Scriptures and the God of Abraham, Isaac, and Jacob. His father, about whom little is said, was apparently a cultured Greek (Acts 16:1). Timothy could skillfully confront either Jew or Greek in his ministry and Paul asked him to be circumcised for the benefit of those in the all-important synagogue mission (Acts 16:3).

From then on, Timothy was found traveling with the apostle or visiting and encouraging the various churches as Paul's representative. As long as Paul lived, Timothy was frequently mentioned in connection with him either in person or by letter.

Paul thought he was somewhat timid. Of course, next to the volatile apostle any one of us might seem a bit retiring. It was said of Paul that he was turning the world upside down (Acts 17:6). Timothy had the disadvantage of youth and was hesitant to assert himself to a desirable degree in his care of the churches. Paul urged him to overcome this by setting an example in every aspect of the ministry:

Let no man despise thy youth; but be
thou an example of the believers, in
word, in conversation, in charity, in
spirit, in faith, in purity (1 Timothy
4:12).

Timothy had a difficult calling. The church universal and the local churches needed to expand and prosper in a generally hostile environment. The world is no place for the church, after all, and special efforts would have to be made constantly to keep it strong and vital. Not only did Paul need Timothy's help, but Timothy would have to gather around himself faithful brothers in the Lord so that they could teach others. The aging Paul made the point in one of his last letters, the second letter to Timothy:

And the things that thou hast heard of me among
many witnesses, the same commit thou to faithful
men, who shall be able to teach others also (2 Tim.
2:2).

The faith that was passed from Jesus to the apostles would now be passed on from generation to generation of faithful leaders until the Lord returned for His bride, the church.

The Elders and Deacons

Until the death of John, around 100 A.D., the highest office in the church had been that of apostle. Now two other offices are described in the Scriptures that would continue beyond the apostolic period and throughout the church age. The callings of elder and deacon, with all their special requirements, now enter the biblical record. Paul instructed Timothy and Titus to appoint with care these leaders in the local churches.

The office of elder had several names and facets. It was also called bishop, and included the ministry of the pastor or shepherd, who would feed the flock. The spiritual oversight of the ministry of the churches was commissioned to the elders. They were to be men of unquestioned spiritual maturity and integrity. An actual list of characteristics is given in the Scriptures (1 Timothy 3:1–7 and Titus 1:5–9):

1. Monogamous—a one-wife man
2. Moderate and level headed in temperament
3. Hospitable
4. Capable teacher
5. Not a drunkard, hot tempered, greedy, or pugnacious
6. Patient with others
7. Rules his own house and children well
8. Not a new believer in Christ
9. Have a good reputation among unbelievers

Of course, no one is perfect, and all of us would fall short in one or more of these attributes at one time or another. But these are the general characteristics we should expect in the spiritual leaders of the church. If they don't fit this overall pattern, they should not be considered for the elder position, although they might be able to serve the Lord in many other ways.

The other office, that of deacon (meaning servant) differed in its spiritual aspect. The deacon was certainly supposed to be a highly spiritual man but he did not have the responsibility of spiritual leadership. He was commissioned primarily to look after the physical needs of the church.

The first mention of deacons, which provides a prime example, was in the church at Jerusalem. Circumstances called for the church to feed meals to large crowds, and it was noted that some of the widows were being neglected. Seven deacons were selected and appointed to that problem. The arrangement allowed the apostles to devote their time and attention to prayer and the Word and not be distracted by this important but secondary problem (Acts 6:1–4).

The qualifications for a deacon were similar to those for an elder but were not quite as exacting (1 Timothy 3:8–12):

1. Serious minded
2. Honest and forthright
3. Not a drunkard or greedy
4. Evaluated in a trial period
5. Have serious minded wife, who is not a gossip
6. Monogamous
7. Rules his family well

Again, these are general traits that should characterize a deacon when he is selected and as he directs the affairs of the church's various ministries. We must keep in mind that the entire church is composed of convicted sinners.

Thus there was a division of labor between what might be called the spiritual ministries and the administrative ministries. The elders saw to the leadership, care of the flock, teaching and preaching, and the deacons were concerned with food, properties, and day-to-day operations of the church. The particular offices and their characteristics were sensible and well suited to the needs of the church. The new people had a pattern to go by since these offices were very much comparable to those of the Rabbi and the Shamas in the synagogues.

The Farewell Address

Inevitably time had run out for the great apostle, a true hero of the faith and one of the most influential men who ever lived. Ready to face trial and execution in Nero's court, Paul sent to his beloved son Timothy his last farewell.

He had modest final requests, including a warm coat and some books and parchments (2 Timothy 4:13). He was surely not one to lament his earthly fate, and along with the occasional personal note, he continued to teach to the end. The awesome breadth of his vision becomes apparent in his warnings to Timothy about the last days of the church age. Some of the corrupt developments of his time would persist, he said, and become still worse near the end:

This know also, that in the last days
perilous times shall come.

For men shall be lovers of their own
selves, covetous, boasters, proud,
blasphemers, disobedient to parents,
unthankful, unholy.

Without natural affection, trucebreakers,
false accusers, incontinent, fierce,
despisers of those that are good.

Traitors, heady, highminded, lovers of
pleasures more than lovers of God:

Having a form of godliness, but denying
the power thereof: from such turn away.

For of this sort are they which creep
into houses, and lead captive silly
women laden with sins, led away with
divers lusts,

> Ever learning, and never able to come to
> the knowledge of the truth (2 Timothy
> 3:1–7).

We, who live in such times as Paul describes above, can appreciate his foresight. He was a prophet to rank with Isaiah, an enlightened and informed leader to rank with Solomon, an unaffected repentant sinner like David, and a servant of longsuffering like Jeremiah. The church has seen many a splendid leader since Paul, but the Romans put to death a man who has no equal.

The New Jews
(Hebrews, James, Peter)

The first Christians, the Jews of Israel and elsewhere, were experiencing special problems in their walk with the Lord. They had been raised with the synagogue, the priesthood, Temple worship and intense loyalty to their very special people and nation. Faith in Christ represented a true change of life for them.

Furthermore, within a generation after Christ Israel was torn apart by the Roman destruction of Jerusalem and the Temple, and the resulting dispersion of the Jewish people throughout the Empire. Jesus had prophesied this calamity and warned His followers to escape it, and so the Jewish Christians experienced conflict between the evident truthfulness of their Messiah and the welfare of their country.

The struggle was duly recognized in the New Testament, and the Spirit of God inspired four epistles particularly designed to help and counsel the new Jews, the Jewish Christians.

A Higher Priest

In the Epistle to the Hebrews, Jesus Christ is cited as a superior priest, more effective than the priesthood of the

Temple. The receivers of this letter were comfortable conceiving of Jesus in His priestly role.

The author and the addressees of Hebrews are not known for certain. Many assume Paul wrote the Epistle, but the author claims only a second-hand knowledge of Christ, whereas Paul had always stressed his direct relationship to the Messiah (Hebrews 2:3; Galatians 1:11–12). Possibly the author was the well-studied Apollos, whose expertise in the Old Testament had led many a Jew to his Messiah (Acts 18:24–28). As to the recipients of the letter, we can well imagine that they were the believers in Jerusalem, who would have been particularly tempted to return to the Levitical priesthood and the worship of the Almighty in the Temple. The Epistle most carefully draws the differences between the faith in the Messiah and the Old Covenant manner of worship.

The courageous Jewish Christians of Jerusalem had been putting their lives on the line for their faith. Peter and John had been jailed there, and Stephen and James had suffered martyrdom. Paul was arrested in the Temple courtyard on the occasion of his visit with Trophimus. And earlier on, Paul himself had led the determined coalition in the Sanhedrin that was zealously committed to stamping out every vestige of Jewish Christianity.

Moreover, Jerusalem was the pure expression of the highest and best of Judaism. For over a thousand years the Law of Moses had been honored there; King David made his capital there; the two Temples of God had been constructed and reconstructed there on Mount Moriah; the revered prophets had proclaimed the special messages of God from that citadel of worship; the descendants of the tribe of Levi still officiated in their roles as priests, offering sacrifices to the One True God, and most important of all, the people of Israel knew that the promised Messiah was coming to

Jerusalem. The hopes and dreams of all Israel rested on Jerusalem, the Golden City, the chosen earthly home of God. The history of magnificent bygone ages of Judaism could be excavated there (as is being done even today), and the very essence of all that was Jewish was somehow contained in that unique and sacred place. How odd and how divisive it was, then, for the Jewish believers in Jesus to break away from that glorious tradition and attach themselves to a Nazarene carpenter who had been condemned for blasphemy.

But boldly, the writer of Hebrews explains to the troubled recipients that the true Messiah is greater than the prophets, greater than Moses, greater than the angels, and certainly greater than the human priests of the Temple. On the last point Jesus was more than a priest like the Levites, but a priest like Melchizedek, the writer explains. The primary thrust of the letter is the expounding of Christ's greater priesthood predicted in Psalms 110:4 (Hebrews 5:6). The two terms particularly developed in this Messianic prophecy are *forever* and *Melchizedek*.

The Levitical priests were obviously not forever. They died and had to be replaced by their descendants. The high priest was consistently replaced and the work he did was never finished. He was commissioned to make the ultimate sacrifice of each year on the Day of Atonement (Leviticus 16), but obviously God was never fully satisfied with this ministry as it had to be repeated annually. The sacrifice of Christ, however, is for always. He is the Eternal Priest. Though He died, His death was only temporary and He rose again to enter into His intercessory ministry as our Great High Priest (Hebrews 7:24–25). Unlike any earthbound priest, however sincere, Christ's priestly ministry is effective forever.

The death of Christ was the one completely satisfying

sacrifice for sin. It was "once for all" (Hebrews 10:10–12). It never has to be repeated. God's righteousness was utterly satisfied with the one priestly offering of His sinless Son.

In addition to the everlasting nature of Christ's priesthood, the writer shows that He is a superior priest because he is of the "order of Melchizedek." Out of the dim past the Psalmist and now the Epistle writer select Melchizedek as the representative type of the Messianic priesthood.

In a very real sense Melchizedek was Abraham's priest long before the establishment of the Levitical priesthood. Abraham paid tithes to Melchizedek who then blessed Abraham (Hebrews 7:4–7). All of this indicated that Melchizedek was Abraham's superior in his priestly ministry. The writer reasons that since Levi was a descendant of Abraham, then Levi too, the father of the Levitical priesthood, recognized Melchizedek's superiority and paid tithes to him through his ancestor Abraham (Hebrews 7:9–11). Thus Melchizedek was priest over Levi, and since the Messiah is in Melchizedek's order, then the Messiah is superior to the priesthood descended from Levi.

The importance of the foregoing technicalities was to stress that the followers of Jesus were not going after some unauthorized rabbi from Galilee, but rather were devotees of the same priesthood as was Abraham. Or in brief, if the Jewish people respected the priesthood, then they should respect the highest of the priests. The struggling Hebrew Christians in Jerusalem and elsewhere should not consider deserting Christ for the Temple and the Levitical priesthood because what they have in Christ is infinitely better.

After making this strong point about the priesthood of Christ, the writer concludes by encouraging his readers to emulate the faith of their ancestors. No matter what the cost they should please God with faith equal to that of the great heroes of the Old Testament, who are enumerated in Hebrews 11. Their faith had always saved them, and now faith in the Messiah was all that any Jew needed.

Faith and Works

James wrote with brevity and force about the nature of true faith. The Jews had long practiced a religion of works, quite properly prior to the coming of the Messiah. But now things were different.

James' salutation puts to rest the theory of the "ten lost tribes." The book is addressed "to the twelve tribes of Israel" (James 1:1) proving that God had not lost them anywhere. Numbers of Jews throughout the ages had been lost in dispersions and captivity, of course, but the tribal system was still intact, at least until the destruction of the Temple and its records in 70 A.D.

Paul had presented previously that it is faith and faith alone that brings us into a right relationship with God. Faith and only faith brings salvation. But James was concerned about the life of the believer *after* his salvation. Did his profession of faith in Christ have a desirable affect on his life? Was he now different? Was his faith evident in his actions?

James stressed that a true life of faith was evidenced by patience in suffering and tribulations, the controlled use of the tongue with all of its ramifications, and genuine helpfulness, such as assisting widows and orphans in their difficulties (James 1:27).

This was the kind of faith father Abraham had, James reasoned. Abraham's faith produced works. He was even willing to sacrifice his own son, Isaac, as evidence of his faith in God and His Word (James 2:21–23).

The Suffering in Christ

Peter, the Galilean fisherman, was deeply concerned about the suffering of his people for their faith. He had, after all, been commissioned by the Lord to "feed the flock" (John 21:17) and to be a minister of the circumcision. The difficult position of the Hebrew Christians commanded much of this important apostle's attention.

He counseled his brethren to remember the extreme suffering of the Messiah as they endured their own sufferings and to follow His godly and perfect example. He had stood beside the Lord Himself in the Garden of Gethsemane and even tried to protect Him from His arrest. He remembered well how Jesus stood as a lamb led before the shearers, silent when he was judged by the Sanhedrin and the Romans in fulfillment of the Scriptures (John 21:17). Believers of all times should not be surprised if their lot is to suffer as the Master suffered, and they should not complain about it. The persecution of the godly is an old, old story reaching back to the beginning of the Bible itself.

Neither will material gains in this life count for anything when the Lord returns. The believer need not seek comforts on earth because these will be ultimately of no effect. Astute in the area of prophecy, Peter reviews the end of the age with his readers in his second letter. He says that the Lord is delaying His return out of mercy, evidently so that God can call out all possible souls to salvation. But when He does return all the material wealth people strive for will be burned up (2 Peter 3:7, 10–12). In view of the final abolishment of the material things, Peter urges us to live lives devoted to the Lord in every aspect.

Worship, Faith and Suffering

Clearly the Epistles to the Jewish Christians are of value to the entire church in any age. Some of the problems discussed were special to the unique situations of the Israelites, but the impact of the letters is also universal (which of us, Jew or Gentile, appreciates with real understanding the ways of proper worship?) Since the Old Covenant is the foundation of the New, and since the actions of the Jews of the Old Testament are given as examples for us all, then the intricate explanations of the book of Hebrews are of enormous importance. Likewise James' explanation of the right relationship of faith and works deals with a problem typical of the church of any age. Finally, Peter's compassionate counsel on the heaviness of the burden of the cross invariably concerns us all. His final remarks on the end of the age have prepared the church of each generation to remain in a posture of spiritual readiness.

A proper reading of the epistles to the Jewish Christians provides not only an understanding of the difficulties faced by a particular people at a particular time, but a compassionate understanding of the difficulties facing the believers of all times.

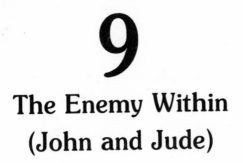

The Enemy Within
(John and Jude)

Living with Roman paganism, Greek sophism, and Israeli legalism was a foregone conclusion for the church. We have already seen how these worldly outside influences affected the thinking of the early Christians. But more serious, professing believers *within* the church were tempted to doctrines and practices that could cause its collapse.

In Paul's farewell address to the elders of the Ephesian church he warned of the wolves who would come to destroy the flock from within (Acts 20:29). In some ways the church had more to fear from its own than from the coming and going philosophies of outsiders. Critical errors began to appear within the ranks of the believers just as Paul had expected.

The Apostle John picked up this theme in the latter years of his long life. As an apostle and as an observer of Christ, he was now a venerable observer of a multitude of church bodies. He wrote three dynamically useful letters primarily to warn the congregations about the enemy within.

Sinless Perfection

Some people thought that a believer in Christ could achieve total sinlessness:

> If we say that we have no sin, we
> deceive ourselves, and the truth is
> not in us (1 John 1:8).

Evidently some in the church claimed to be so holy that they had eradicated all vestiges of their old sin natures. They neither practiced nor possessed sin in any form. Considerable dissension came to the church through their "holier than thou" attitude. The overachievers were deeply resented.

John stated decisively that any person who claims to be without sin in this age simply does not believe God. The Word of God is explicit in the Almighty's evaluation of the human sin nature. When we receive Christ we do receive a new nature that is spiritually alive, but we also continue to carry around the old nature that is spiritually dead. The two natures are in continual conflict, and because of that the believer experiences a war within himself (Romans 7:20–23). Therefore, believers often sin against the Lord in thought, word, or action, and if we don't recognize that fact we are very seriously deceived. But there is a clear remedy for this problem:

> If we confess our sins, he is faithful
> and just to forgive us our sins, and to
> cleanse us from all unrighteousness (1 John 1:9).

By merely confessing our sins to God, we receive complete forgiveness and cleansing. It is that simple. The broken lines of fellowship with the Lord are restored, and spiritual vitality continues.

While the procedure is simple, it is not always painless. For us to acknowledge our sins, in general and in particular, is frequently a difficult experience that wounds our own pride and high opinion of ourselves. The humility required for us to make a clean breast of things with God is not easily attained. But confess we must, and when we do we experience the spiritual rejuvenation that God has promised.

Insecurity

Another group of teachers seemed to capitalize on the doubts of the believers. They were saying it was presumptuous for anyone to declare dogmatically that he has eternal life.

How could a human being know he is saved? And even if we feel that we are saved for now, isn't it possible for us to do something later on that would cause us to lose our salvation? Many Christians listened to these seemingly reasonable questions and began to doubt the reality and permanence of their redemption. They were becoming insecure in their faith.

John responded vigorously to these doubts and those who were fostering them. He pointed out that our salvation is not dependent on *our* faithfulness but on *God's* faithfulness, and upon that faithfulness we can rest—assured. All man can do in the process of salvation is to receive by faith the Son of God:

> And this is the record, that God hath given
> to us eternal life, and this life is in his Son.
>
> He that hath the Son hath life; and he that hath
> not the Son of God hath not life (1 John 5:11–12).

If all man is required to do for salvation is receive Christ, then once that is done we can humbly but dogmatically proclaim that we have eternal life. No power in heaven, hell, or earth can destroy a man's salvation.

John also supplied several evidences that prove to ourselves and others that we have genuinely received Christ. It is a characteristic of the Christian, he said, to "love the brethren" (1 John 3:14). If we enjoy a special relationship with our fellow brothers and sisters in the Lord, seeking their fellowship and companionship, it is a good sign of true salvation. If we shun the fellowship of believers, it is a sign that we never have received Christ. Another sign of valid salvation is simply doing what Christ commands (1 John 5:2). We may fail often in our old natures, but if the true desire of our hearts is to follow the Master in all that He has instructed, this is excellent evidence of our redemption. Those who consider the Lord's Word irrelevant or inconsequential only proclaim to themselves, the church, and the world that they are not genuine believers. Obviously John does not teach that an individual can be saved by merely loving the brethren or keeping Christ's commands. These are rather the evidences of true salvation and invariably accompany the walk of the true believer.

The Spirit of the Antichrist

We discussed above the heresy called Gnosticism which attacked both the deity and humanity of Christ. Both Paul and John wrote strong responses to this distortion. John went so far as to say that if an individual taught that Jesus Christ was not fully human, he was to be considered a false teacher, imbued with the spirit of the Antichrist:

Hereby know ye the Spirit of God: Every
spirit that confesseth that Jesus Christ
is come in the flesh is of God:

And every spirit that confesseth not that
Jesus Christ is come in the flesh is not
of God: and this is that spirit of antichrist,
whereof ye have heard that it should come;
and even now already is it in the world
(1 John 4:2–3).

(See also 2 John 7.)

We will deal with the Antichrist in the following chapter on the Book of Revelation. The satanic individual has not presented himself as yet, but his spirit and philosophy have been with us for thousands of years. The spirit of the Antichrist is that which diminishes Christ and exalts mankind. It exists profusely in the world and to some measure in the church. The believer is warned to be constantly on guard concerning this vital issue and to test the spirits of people to see if they are really of God or Satan. Believers in Christ are obligated to receive, foster, and encourage those who teach the truth about the Lord and His Word; we are just as strongly to shun those who bring false teachings (3 John 5–11). In this manner the true church, if each believer is discharging his obligation, should consistently be cleansed of false doctrine.

Preaching for Profit

Jude wrote a short but fiery attack on false teachers in his one-chapter book. A brother of Jesus, like James, he was deeply concerned about the motives of the false teachers and their disastrous impact on the churches:

> For there are certain men crept in unawares,
> who were before of old ordained to this
> condemnation, ungodly men, turning the grace
> of our God into lasciviousness, and denying
> the only Lord God, and our Lord Jesus Christ
> (Jude 4).

False doctrine results in false living. Teaching and actions cannot be separated. The behavior of any people springs from what they understand, teacher and disciples alike.

Jude did not gift-wrap his message or take time for tact and diplomacy. He made himself most clear about the false teachers, comparing them to some of the most nefarious characters in the Old Testament. They are like Cain, who murdered his brother Abel out of spiritual jealousy; they are like Balaam, who uttered prophecies for monetary gain; they are like Core, who disputed Moses' authority as a man of God:

> Woe unto them! for they have gone in the way
> of Cain, and ran greedily after the error of
> Balaam for reward, and perished in the gain-
> saying of Core (Jude 11).

Thus again, as in the Epistles of John, we are warned to have nothing to do with these people or their teachings. The struggle, of course, goes on, since false teaching hardly died with the first century church. As in ancient days the believers, to maintain doctrinal purity, must stand clearly against the false teachers while at the same time loving and caring for the true brethren.

Jude concludes his exhortations and entire body of the epistles with one of the most serene and elegant doxologies in Scripture:

> Now unto him that is able to keep you from
> failing, and to present you faultless before
> the presence of his glory with exceeding joy,
>
> To the only wise God our Saviour, be glory and
> majesty, dominion and power, both now and ever.
> Amen (Jude 24–25).

10

From Here to Eternity
(Revelation)

"The Revelation of Jesus Christ" is the capstone of the entire Bible. It draws together all the threads of the Old Testament and New, all the prophecies, promises, warnings, and blessings into a dramatic climax.

Revelation contains manifold information for those who earnestly study the Word of God and desire to understand it, but it is virtually inexplicable to those untaught in biblical interpretation. Unbelievers and casual Bible readers alike find its symbolism and imagery opaque. A forbidding maze of unfamiliar figures and pictures awaits those who have little Bible background, but, to the initiated, Revelation presents a beautiful culmination of the biblical themes. Those who believe with child-like faith the events recorded in Genesis and Daniel find the messages of Revelation clear and satisfying.

The writer is the Apostle John, now exiled to the barren island of Patmos for his faith. The book was written at the close of the first century, close to the end of John's life. The writer was honored with a vision of the glorified Christ in all of His power and majesty and then faithfully recorded the things he heard and saw (Revelation 1:19).

The Church: Then and Now

The Lord begins His Revelation by addressing the new people, the Church. He selects seven representative churches in Asia Minor in which Paul and John had labored for most of their lives. The Lord dictates a message to each church, praising and criticizing them and giving them warnings and promises. The praises range from commendations for faithfulness, sound doctrine, and true brotherly love, even in persecution. The criticisms deal with the loss of the "first love," going after false teachers and doctrines, and the pretense of spirituality in the presence of carnality.

The praises ring with warmth and love and the indictments are given in the severest terms. The warnings to the churches mainly have to do with their losing their light of witness for Christ and the promises deal with the rewards to be given the faithful in eternity (Revelation 2:10, 17). The several messages are somewhat similar in content to the epistles, but have the added weight of coming from the lips of the Lord Himself.

They were real churches in real cities with real problems, but they stand for more than that. They are representative of local churches throughout the age. Some churches today reflect the dynamic witness for Christ that the church in Philadelphia was commended for, while others are full of material wealth, hypocrisy, and worldliness in the manner of the Laodicean congregation. The seven messages comprise a word to the wise in evaluating the state of the current church. The Lord's words, here as in the Gospels, are uncannily relevant to the human condition of any age.

In addition, the messages to the seven churches seem to describe a prophetic system of the various phases of church history. Many Bible teachers have observed that the order given in Revelation, with the distinctive evaluations, closely parallels the experience of the church since the first century. Beginning with the church struggling in persecution to the compromises made with Rome, to the dark days of the Middle Ages, to the Reformation with its resultant surge of world-wide evangelism, to the unspiritual and indolent church of the last days, the Lord's words are prophetic. We have played out over nearly two millenia the hopes and dreams, the sins and frustrations of our earliest brothers and sisters of the church.

When the messages are finished John is taken to heaven for further revelation. It is implied at this point that the church age is over in the prophetic scheme of things, and John now represents the final church which is raptured before God's terrible judgments on the world. The church will go in resurrection glory to the Judgment Seat of Christ where we will receive rewards for what we have done in His service (2 Corinthians 5:10; 1 Corinthians 3:11–15). The resurrected church will be married to Christ in a heavenly ceremony, completing those lovely images of Christ and the believers as Groom and Bride (Revelation 19:7–8).

The destiny of the true church is magnificent according to the biblical record. But the destiny of the unbeliever is tragic.

The Tribulation

The faithful church is not seen again on earth from this point through the next sixteen chapters. What is now described in the most vivid terms are the events of a seven-year period called the Tribulation. The seven years coincide with Daniel's Seventieth Week and earlier biblical descriptions of the Day of the Lord.

There are two major developments in the course of these climactic seven years:

1. Satan will achieve his age-old dream of gaining virtually complete control over the earth through his false Messiah, the Antichrist.
2. God will pour out His wrath on a world that has despised His Son, will destroy Satan and the Antichrist, and will prepare Israel and some of the Gentiles for Christ's victorious return to earth.

The Beast

Throughout the Revelation the Antichrist is repeatedly described in visions as the Beast:

> And I stood upon the sand of the sea, and saw a beast rise up out of the sea, having seven heads and ten horns, and upon his horns ten crowns, and upon his heads the name of blasphemy (Revelation 13:1)

He is as cunning, ravenous, and destructive as any wild beast of the jungle ever was. He has a helper who is also described as a Beast. The first is the dominant figure who will gain control of the world militarily, economically, and religiously. The second is a False Prophet who will encourage the world to follow the Antichrist.

The Antichrist is apparently a Gentile who has his power base in Europe as sort of a revived Roman Empire. The False Prophet, who arises out of "the land" (Revelation 13:11) may well be a Jew who will be highly influential in getting much of Israel and the world to submit themselves to the leadership of the Antichrist.

The Antichrist will appear to the world to be an angel of

light, a miracle worker with the finest answers to mankind's universal problems. It may well be that his initial thrust to power will be his platform for peace for Israel and the Middle East. He will enter into some kind of a treaty with Israel for seven years (Daniel 9:27). That act will start the countdown for the Tribulation. During these days Israel will fulfill its ancient dream of rebuilding the Temple of God in Jerusalem.

The Antichrist will ascend to power also with the guidance and blessing of the "church." We already explained that the genuine church will be taken to heaven in the Rapture before the Tribulation begins. But there will be a "church" left on earth, all the merely professing followers of Christ who never truly knew Him. This Tribulation Church is described in the most awful terms as a harlot, or in modern terminology, a prostitute:

> So he carried me away in the spirit into
> the wilderness: and I saw a woman sit upon
> a scarlet coloured beast, full of names
> of blasphemy, having seven heads and ten
> horns.
>
> The beast that thou sawest was, and is not;
> and shall ascend out of the bottomless pit,
> and go into perdition: and they that dwell
> on the earth shall wonder, whose names were not
> written in the book of life from the foundation
> of the world, when they behold the beast that
> was, and is not, and yet is.
>
> And the ten horns which thou sawest upon the
> beast, these shall hate the whore, and shall
> make her desolate and naked, and shall eat
> her flesh, and burn her with fire (Revelation
> 17: 3, 8, 16).

Initially, the apostate church will follow the Beast to

power, but after he is firmly in control, the Antichrist will throw off his attachments to the church and destroy it.

The Faithful

The true message of God will still be available in the world even during the terrible time of the Tribulation. One hundred and forty-four thousand Israelites who believe in Christ will proclaim the Gospel throughout all nations:

> And I heard the number of them which were
> sealed: and there were sealed an hundred
> and forty and four thousand of all the
> tribes of the children of Israel (Revelation
> 7:4).

The Jewish evangelists will endure terrible persecution, but they will also see some success. Many do not appreciate that the Tribulation is a time of salvation as well as an awesome time of punishment. The Lord will return to separate the sheep from the goats—the Tribulation period believers from the unbelievers (Matthew 25:31–46). Their faith will cost them their lives since the Antichrist will be bent on eliminating those who do not identify themselves with him (Revelation 13:16–18).

Abomination and Armageddon

Evidently the Antichrist will finally overreach himself. At the zenith of his power he will resent the independence of the nation of Israel, who never bow to dictators, and he will enter the rebuilt Temple of Jerusalem. He will claim that he is God Himself and he will demand the worship of the Jews and the world (2 Thessalonians 2:3–4; Revelation 13:15).

Daniel and Jesus refer to this "Abomination of Desolation" (Daniel 9:27; Matthew 24:15).

Israel, which has been fairly accepting of the various postures of the Antichrist up to this point, will find it impossible to tolerate this madness. They will declare open revolt against the Antichrist, much as they did against Antiochus in the ancient days of the Macabees. Antiochus too, tried to take over the Temple and finally met his match.

From then on there is determined hostility between the Antichrist and Israel. He persecutes the Jewish people unmercifully until they can scarcely find refuge anywhere (Revelation 12:13–17). He is determined to wipe out any vestige of the Chosen People and their perpetual testimony to the Almighty. He joins the satanic company of a long line of voracious oppressors of the Jews: Pharoah, Nebuchadnezzar, Titus, Hadrian, the Crusaders, the Inquisitors, and the peerless Hitler.

Ultimately this hostility leads to the mightiest of wars: the Antichrist with the armies of the world against little Israel and the Lord. It is David and Goliath again on a monumental scale.

The Salvation of Israel

But the Lord will return to put a stop to the bloody work of Armageddon. Just at Israel's darkest hour the entire Jewish nation will turn in faith to God and the Messiah Jesus Christ. When the Lord returns, the age-old blindness will be lifted:

> And so all Israel shall be saved: as it
> is written, There shall come out of Sion
> the Deliverer, and shall turn away
> ungodliness from Jacob: (Romans 11:26). See
> also Zechariah 12:10; 13:1.

The Lord will make short work of destroying the satanic armies and establishing His long-promised kingdom on earth.

"Thy Kingdom Come"

The inhabitants of Christ's kingdom will be the glorified saints of the Old Testament and Church ages, saved Israel, and the "sheep"—Gentiles who believed in the message of the 144,000 Jewish Christian preachers and treated them well (Matthew 25:31-34, 40). It will be an interesting mixture of resurrected and mortal believers who will occupy the earth, restored to Edenic conditions, while the Lord reigns for a thousand years:

> And I saw thrones, and they sat upon them,
> and judgment was given unto them: and I
> saw the souls of them that were beheaded
> for the witness of Jesus, and for the word
> of God, and which had not worshipped the
> beast, neither his image, neither had
> received his mark upon their foreheads,
> or in their hands; and they lived and
> reigned with Christ a thousand years
> (Revelation 20:4).

But even the millenium will not last forever, and once the Lord has accomplished His purposes for this present earth, He will terminate the kingdom age. Then will come the time for the dramatic final judgment at the Great White Throne. All the unbelieving dead will be raised to be judged and cast into the Lake of Fire with Satan forever:

> And I saw a great white throne, and him
> that sat on it, from whose face the earth
> and the heaven fled away; and there was
> found no place for them.

> And whosoever was not found written in the
> book of life was cast into the lake of fire
> (Revelation 20:11, 15).

Once that difficult and sad task is over, the Lord will turn His attention to His own, and will create the New Heaven, the New Earth, and the New Jerusalem. These will be the eternal abode of the humble believers in Christ. John's description of the New Jerusalem is a study in how difficult it must be to write about heavenly glories in earthly language. Nevertheless, the word picture he paints is stunningly attractive to all believers:

> And I John saw the holy city, new Jerusalem,
> coming down from God out of heaven, prepared
> as a bride adorned for her husband (Revelation
> 21:2).

"Come, Lord Jesus"

Thus the New Testament, and the entire biblical Revelation, ends with a new beginning. Nothing can be written about eternity to explain it to us because it is beyond our grasp. We know only that we are back to the mysterious circumstance in which there is no time. The Bible deals only with the thing called Time which separates eternity past from eternity future. What God has accomplished is a solution for His aloneness. God was totally alone in eternity past, but in eternity future He will have with Him those who love Him.

The true believer is in great discomfort in this world. One thing that the Revelation of Jesus Christ reveals is that we have not improved upon the circumstances of the churches of the first century. In some ways we have deteriorated because the world itself has spiritually deteriorated. The truth of the Book of Revelation seems more and more apparent as the unbelieving world degenerates. "Armageddon" has become a coined term of political journalism; accurately enough it refers to some coming final conflict seemingly now in the making.

Were it not for the promises of the Bible and their outworkings, as presented in Revelation, the believer would be in difficult straits. He would have no hope, just as the unbeliever has no hope in God's final judgment. But instead God has chosen to reveal in finest detail the ultimate conclusions of all of His plans, and the believers can count on the brightest of all possible futures.

That is why we still pray with John after nineteen centuries, "Even so, come, Lord Jesus."

PART 2
The Continuing Drama

11

Prophecy Fulfilled

If the Bible were compared to a dramatic production, the New Testament writers were in the second act of a three-act play. The Old Testament, with its unique personalities, events, prophecies, and promises, represents the first act. Act two was centered around Christ and the Church He created. Act three will be the resolution of the drama with the Lord returning to accomplish all the unfulfilled prophecies made by the ancient Hebrew Prophets, Himself, and the Apostles.

In any good drama the conclusion ties up all the loose ends given throughout the play, and thus readers of the Bible can look at the future with a special satisfaction. The accuracy with which the first advent of Christ fulfilled the appropriate prophecies in the Old Testament is a prediction of the certainty of the nature of the second advent. We can confidently describe things to come with the Bible as our tool, and in the continuing drama each reader can consider himself and his life as a part of God's magnificent drama about time and eternity. Prophecy, fulfilled and unfulfilled, gives us a sense of our place in the unfolding saga of God's mighty works. We all make our entrances at some given point with regard to the prophecies, and as believers we remain on the stage forever.

Every New Testament writer, without exception, quoted Old Testament prophecies as having been fulfilled. They knew that the Messiah, God's anointed One, had finally come, and they rejoiced that in every aspect of His first coming He did the things the prophets of Israel had indicated.

The Seed of the Woman

We alluded in our opening chapters to the identifying prophecies about the Messiah. He has a very definite physical bloodline extending from the Garden of Eden to His birth in Bethlehem. One of the major themes of God's drama is the "manhunt" that unfolds as the human genealogy of the Messiah is continuously revealed. We will occasionally be repeating prophecies referred to in the opening chapters as we trace these important revelations.

The earliest Messianic prophecy is given in the first pages of the Bible while our parents, Adam and Eve, were still in the Garden of Eden. The need for a redeemer arose when they sinned and God told them that "the seed of the woman" would crush the "head of the serpent" (Genesis 3:15). Clearly someone was to come sooner or later to destroy Satan and the power he had gained over the human race.

Centuries passed and the flood came and went before God spoke again on the matter of the Messiah. One of Noah's sons, Shem, was designated as part of the Messianic line (Genesis 9:26). We could now eliminate the millions of descendants of Ham and Japheth, Noah's other sons, from the lineage of the Promised One.

More centuries passed and the Tower of Babel with its inherent insult to God came and went. Seemingly as an immediate reaction, God called forth a descendant of Shem, one of the dominant actors in our cosmic drama, Abraham of Ur. God transformed Abraham from a sophisticated citizen of the idolotrous Euphrates Valley to a nomad shepherd in the hilly land of the Canaanites. He promised to this wandering one that through him would come the promised Seed and also a great nation and land. The entire world would ultimately be blessed through the Seed of Abraham (Genesis 12:1–3).

The obedient Abraham and his wife Sarah left the comforts of the Chaldean home in answer to God's promises. Abraham lived to see the birth of Isaac, the continuation of the covenant with God, but died before the birth of Isaac's twins, Jacob and Esau. We should appreciate that all that Abraham had in return for his life of faith was a son who himself would not live to see even the promise of the land fulfilled. The three generations of patriarchs wandered as nomads with their tents, and the only part of the Promised Land they possessed were the graveyards they purchased to bury their dead.

Some four centuries later, though, the land part of God's promise to Abraham became a reality. Moses led the descendants of the patriarchs out of Egypt, and Joshua brought them as conquerors into the Promised Land. Then God issued additional information about the Seed and his lineage.

In Jacob's old age, that last one of the patriarchs prophesied that of his twelve sons, Judah would possess the royal scepter for the nation (Genesis 49:10). It was from Judah's line that the ultimate King would come. Now, ten generations after Judah, David of Bethlehem was anointed by the prophet Samuel to be the founder of the eternal royal dynasty (2 Samuel 7:16). We have already discussed how the divine program unfolded with regard to the Messiah's royal line. It was clear now that the original "seed of the woman" which had come through Seth, Noah, Shem, Abraham, and Judah, must eventually be sought in the descendancy of the house of King David.

We stand now at a point about one thousand years before the arrival of the Messiah, and the prophecies narrow down to definite characteristics of His birth and ministry.

The Signs of His Coming

It was not enough for God just to give the physical blood-line of the Messiah. Conceivably some pretender to the Messianic calling could arise from David's line and lay false claim to the unique distinction. And so the Lord revealed as well precise details about the time, place, and nature of the birth of the Messiah and additional information about His earthly ministry.

We already discussed in the opening chapters Jesus' Virgin Birth (Isaiah 7:14). In the context of prophecy we might point out that it answered beautifully to that cryptic "seed of the woman" expression in Genesis 3:15. It came translated as virgin, and Isaiah's verse has been disputed by scholars, but it is evident that the ancient Jews considered it to mean exactly that because they translated it that way in their Greek Septuageint version over a century before Christ.

As to the place of birth, we also have already cited Micah's prophecy about Bethlehem. In this prophetic context we can see that it was entirely fitting for God to choose the very birthplace of King David. It should be noted that Bethlehem is an insignificant little village, or as Micah put it, "little among the thousands of Judah." The Messiah might have been expected out of Jerusalem. Big places held significance to the Jewish people and Jesus was faulted for being raised in Galilee, unlike most of the prophets. But then it may have given many Old Testament readers pause to reflect that the hamlet of Bethlehem, a mere bend in the road in the Judaean hills, had brought forth the mighty David. We should note too, in the context of discussing prophecy, that Micah was not speaking of an ordinary man; as a matter of fact, His "goings forth have been from of old, from everlasting" (Micah 5:2).

The time of the Messiah's coming is established in Daniel's mighty "Seventy Weeks of Years" prophecy (Daniel 9:24–27). Space does not permit a thorough analysis of that prediction, but it is easy to see at a glance that sixty-nine of Daniel's "Weeks of Years" did indeed describe the time of Jesus' coming. That period was to pass between Artaxerxes' commandment to restore and rebuild Jerusalem (Nehemiah 2:1–6) and the coming of the Promised One. The period totals 476 years on the Hebrew calendar, and since Artaxerxes' commandment was issued in 445 B.C., then the Messiah had to come in the first generation of the first century A.D. Sir Robert Anderson, a British astronomer of a century ago, computed in his work *The Coming Prince* that Daniel's prediction came out to the exact *day* of Jesus' entry into Jerusalem on the donkey!

With the place of birth and the time and the feature of the virgin mother, all possibility of a pretender was eliminated. If the Old Testament Scriptures are to be believed, Jesus Christ is the Messiah of Israel.

But God went on, giving details about the earthly ministry through particularly Isaiah and Zechariah. Jesus Himself told His home synagogue in Nazareth that the magnificent verses Isaiah 61:1–2a were being fulfilled before their very eyes in His ministry. The Lord told Zechariah to enact the role of a shepherd whose work was despised by the people; it was a dramatic portrayal of the rejection of the Messiah (Zechariah 11:4, 10–12). The people would consider the ministry of the shepherd worth no more than the value of a slave—a thought provoking picture of thirty pieces of silver.

Death and Resurrection

The most unlikely prophecies about the Messiah, if one thinks about it, are those that concern His death. Why should the Messiah die after all? Yet the Seed of the woman, the Rebuker of Satan, the Lion of Judah, the Son of David was prophesied to be rejected by the world and Israel and to die as a common criminal. All this was revealed to Isaiah in his incomparable 53rd chapter.

Isaiah perceived that the Servant of the Lord would be despised and rejected (Isaiah 53:3), that He would die with thieves and yet be associated with the wealthy in His death (Isaiah 53:9), but that also God would consider His death to be an offering for sin and would provide substitutionary atonement (Isaiah 53:6, 10).

Even King David himself, who suffered quite a bit in his early days while he was being persecuted by a jealous and vengeful Saul, wrote in the Psalms about the terrible sufferings of the Messiah. Psalm 22 describes in vivid detail the separation of the Messiah from God and how His hands and feet were pierced (Psalms 22:16).

But David also saw the resurrection of God's divinely-ordained Son, and prophesied that the soul of the Holy One would not remain in Sheol and His body would not see corruption. The Messiah was to be gloriously raised from the dead (Psalm 16:10).

Again, we must apologize for the brevity of the coverage of this subject. There are hundreds of prophecies, types, illustrations and so forth throughout the Old Testament that ingeniously describe the career of Jesus Christ. We have tried to lay stress on an important few which prove the validity of the New Testament reportage of the first advent of the Lord.

Types of the Church

There are no prophecies in the Old Testament about the Church. The Church seems to have been God's secret, but a careful reader of the Old Testament Scriptures will discover many pictures and types that the apostles recognized in their writings. Paul particularly exulted in the picture of Eve—part of her husband's body and also his bride. The church, like Eve, is being formed out of the wounds of Christ and being fitted as His bride-to-be made one with Him for eternity (Ephesians 5:25, 31–32).

Many Bible students have seen a similar portrayal of the church in the story of Abraham, Isaac, and Rebecca, although it is not confirmed in the New Testament, Abraham sent his servant to obtain a proper wife for Isaac. The servant bore gifts and when he found Rebecca, she accepted them and was brought to Isaac as his bride (Genesis 24:61–64). The images are of the Father, as Abraham, sending the Holy Spirit, as the Servant, to woo Rebecca, as the Church, to present to the Son as his Bride.

Thus the writers of the New Testament were able to appreciate themselves as part of an unfinished divine drama. Much of the play has been enacted; the New Testament writers had seen many prophecies fulfilled. But of course they were well aware that much had *not* been fulfilled and that a huge and splendorous body of prophecy awaits the return of the Lord Jesus Christ.

We turn now, with great enthusiasm, to those magnificent promises which are yet to be fulfilled.

12

Prophecy Unfulfilled

There always have been those, even within the church, who doubt the validity of biblical prophecy. Some have always felt that there would be no return of the King and no kingdom to come, and that the prophecies are either inexplicably symbolic or simply misunderstood.

The apostles were not among them.

The apostles were among those who could see that the Messiah had fulfilled the hundreds of Old Testament prophecies associated with His coming, His ministry, His death, and His resurrection. But they had no delusions that all prophecy was completed. They were persuaded that the prophecies concerning the King and His kingdom simply awaited the return of Christ.

Nineteen Centuries!

The apostles took Christ at His word, knowing that He would return as He had promised (John 14:3). So they awaited an early coming. But as the time went on and apostles died the new leaders began to realize that the church age was going to last longer than they anticipated. They would have been astonished to know that they were beginning a wait of nineteen centuries to date.

The very length of the church age has caused some to think that the return of Christ is merely the wishful thinking of the believers. But all prophecy, and subsequently all Christianity, would crumble if there were no second advent, no return of the King. Nineteen centuries is not a long period in God's way of doing things; Israel waited longer than that from the promises to Abraham to the first coming of the Messiah. God has promises yet to keep and He has always kept His promises before.

The long wait is, in a subtle way, part of having true faith. It is God's plan to keep us ready and waiting, with lengthy anticipation of this climactic event. Many true believers have lived and died since the Lord left us. Every one of them awaited His return.

There are actually three major phases to the return of Jesus Christ that we should discuss separately: the Rapture, the Second Coming, and the Eternal State.

The Rapture

We touched on the Rapture in our earlier discussion about the new message of the church. In essence, the Rapture is a future event in which the Lord will terminate the church age and take all the believers out of the world. The unbelievers will remain on earth to confront the Tribulation Period, and finally God's final judgment.

> For the Lord himself shall descend from heaven
> with a shout, with the voice of the archangel,
> and with the trump of God: and the dead in
> Christ shall rise first:
>
> Then we which are alive and remain shall be
> caught up together with them in the clouds, to

meet the Lord in the air: and so shall we ever
be with the Lord (1 Thessalonians 4:16–17).

Christ will not return to the earth, per se, but will appear
in the heavens and call His own with a shout and the blast
of a trumpet. The souls of those who have died in Christ
through the centuries of the church age will be reunited with
the remains of their dead bodies, and the bodies will be
resurrected into the same kind of eternal body Jesus had
when He rose from the dead. Those who are still alive will
also be changed completely, taking on immortal bodies and
ascending with the resurrected ones to the Lord's presence
(1 Corinthians 15:51–57). All of this will take place "in the
twinkling of an eye" and once the Lord has assembled His
body, His glorified bride, He will take her across the light
years to His heaven.

Two important events await us in heaven after we are
united with Christ. We mentioned the Judgment Seat in the
chapter on Revelation; there our ministries on earth will be
evaluated to determine the sorts of rewards each of us
earned. This is God's incentive program, as it were, and the
Judgment Seat will reward the endurance of the saints, the
persecutions, the troubles, the sacrifices and all of the good
works done in our bodies (2 Corinthians 5:10). Many will
rejoice over the gold, silver, and precious stones we have
sent ahead, but many will have to reckon with the wood,
hay, and stubble accumulated in their lives (1 Corinthians
3:11–15). The Maker of human nature knows how human
beings operate. We will tend to be more faithful in His
service if there are rewards awaiting us at the end of our
service.

The Marriage Supper of the Lamb, the next event in
heaven, will be a magnificent celebration where the Church
is presented formally to Christ. The Father will perform this
indescribably beautiful ceremony (Revelation 19:7–10) and
all the saints of all ages will rejoice at this ultimate wedding.

Back on earth the Antichrist will have risen to power in the aftermath of the Russian invasion of Israel. He will claim to be God and undertake his persecution of Israel and those who are preaching the Gospel. The unregenerate world will suffer the Tribulation Period while the church enjoys its most glorious seven years to that point.

The Second Coming

The Tribulation, as we have seen, will culminate in the war of Armageddon in which the whole world is involved. The Lord will interrupt this hellish battle with His actual Second Coming to the earth. In the first coming He was the Lamb, sent to be sacrificied. In the Second Coming He is the Lion, sent to rule the world.

He will preserve Israel from certain destruction, judge the nations, and establish His kingdom on earth.

Many Christians dispute the literal kingdom and Christ's personal reign over the whole world. They consider the idea to be carnal and to contradict the teachings of Christ on His kingdom being spiritual and "not of this world" (John 18:36). But here unfulfilled prophecy makes the matter more than clear. There are innumerable prophecies concerning an earthly kingdom that must yet be fulfilled. Jesus taught that the meek will "inherit the earth" (Matthew 5:5) and that the disciples will rule over the twelve tribes of Israel (Matthew 19:28). He confirmed that the kingdom would be restored to Israel, from where He will reign, but he did not reveal the time of the event (Acts 1:6–7).

Furthermore, the Old Testament speaks of Israel being the head of the nations (Deuteronomy 28:13), of all nations flowing into Jerusalem to learn from the Lord (Isaiah 2:1–3), of the knowledge of God covering the earth as the waters cover the ocean (Isaiah 11:9), of nations learning war no more (Isaiah 2:4), and of the wolf and the lamb lying down in peace together (Isaiah 11:6). How will all these prophecies be fulfilled unless Christ returns to the earth and transforms it?

Finally, the length of time of this earthly Kingdom is given in the last book of the Bible. None of the Old Testament or other New Testament books say how long the Messianic reign will last, but in Revelation 20:4–6 we are told several times that it will last a thousand years. Many kings have dreamed of their empires lasting for a thousand years, but only Christ will actually accomplish it.

The Eternal State

The third and final phase of the Lord's return has to do with what theologians call the Eternal State. Just as the Church Age is not forever, neither is the Millennium. As good as the Kingdom Age will be, it is not the best, and the best is yet to come.

The last act of all "time" will be God's judgment of all unrighteous souls. All who have not believed from all ages, from all nations, will be resurrected. They will not be disembodied spirits but will face the Lord in their complete humanity—body, soul, and spirit.

During their lifetime they preferred not to believe, but to rely on themselves and their works. This they will have to do at Christ's Great White Throne. All of their works will be presented in unvarnished truth, and those works in which they trusted will condemn them. All who elected not to be in the Book of Life will be condemned. They will not have the blood of the Lamb to cover their sins and forgive their works. They will be consigned to eternal hell, which is described as the Lake of Fire and the Second Death. It is terribly sad, and no one can or should rejoice over the eternal ruination of the lost. They will be separated from God forever; the judgment is final and beyond recall. Once this awful work is finished, the Lord and His people can turn to the most joyous of all tasks, the establishment of the Eternal Order.

Up to this point the only thing the Lord has made that is physically new since the sixth day of creation is the resurrection body. But the resurrection bodies of Christ and His saints must have a suitable place for such resplendent spiritual and physical beings. So the Lord will create a whole new habitation—the New Heaven, the New Earth, and the New Jerusalem.

Words failed John as he tried to describe the visions of the eternal bliss he saw, and he struggled mightily to do so with divine inspiration. The New Jerusalem, our ultimate home, is of special interest. It will be about 1,500 miles on each side, a square at the base about one-half the size of the United States (Revelation 21:16). It will also be 1,500 miles high, which suggests either a cube or a pyramid in shape. The foundations and gates are designed to insure that we will forever remember the names of the Twelve Apostles and the Twelve Tribes of Israel (Revelation 21:12–14).

Apart from glorifying the Lord we are not told what we will be doing in the New Jerusalem, but we know that our capacity for work, knowledge, and enjoyment will be infinitely greater than it is now.

Unbelievable?

Much of the above is impossible for the unbeliever to appreciate and difficult even for some believers. It is mystical and we have no experience with such goings-on. The only reason we know it will all happen is because God has said so in His infallible Word. We walk by faith, not by sight, just as Abraham did when he wandered in tents looking for a city whose builder and maker is God (Hebrews 11:10).

It is surely not unreasonable to believe the Bible even in its most arcane images. The Book has been tested since its inception and human history has answered precisely to its prophecy and reportage. Personalities and events have come and gone exactly as predicted in the past. It would be unreasonable to disbelieve that the prophecies found in the same book will not be fulfilled to the letter in the future.

The climactic chain of events will begin with the Rapture, and so we continue looking upward for that glorious appearance of our Savior Jesus Christ (Titus 2:13). We see more readily now why the aged John, after having written much of the information above in his startling Revelation of Jesus Christ, could only pray "Come, Lord Jesus."

13

The Development of Doctrine

The Bible was inspired, written, and finished early on, and it is the sole guide for believers in faith and practice. It is regarded by those who read it seriously as complete and inerrant.

But the church's comprehension of the Bible has undergone considerable development throughout the age. Men differ on what they understand by what they read. Every major period of church history has seen its intensive searchings of the Scriptures, often with heated debate, in order to determine what the Bible really intends on some given subject. Four ongoing areas of study include *Ecclesiology*, the church; *Christology*, the nature of Christ; *Soteriology*, salvation; and *Eschatology*, prophecy.

In the church of this age, or any other age, one could pass many a fascinating and sometimes difficult hour in discussion of these primary issues of doctrine. There has been progress through the times as sincere students of the Word have balanced Scripture with Scripture in order precisely to define an ultimate truth. In view of the material treated in God's writing—the very essence of life and death—heaven and earth—there is no more important discussion.

Ecclesiology

One of the first matters the early church had to settle was the nature of its own existence, purpose, and membership. Ecclesiology, or the study of the church, was of prime importance to the apostolic fellowship of the first century.

The several gatherings in Jerusalem to seek the Lord's wisdom about the church had largely to do with the relationship of Jewish and Gentile believers. In church councils the leaders heard practical testimonies, searched the Scriptures, and at length concluded that the church was properly composed of Jewish and Gentile Christians together. Faith in Christ was the only requirement for fellowship in the body. In practice, evangelism to the Jews has not continued with such vigor as at the beginning, but the doctrine arrived at agreed with the Old Testament prophecies about the Messianic age:

> And to this agree the words of the prophets;
> as it is written,
>
> After this I will return, and will build
> again the tabernacle of David, which is fallen
> down; and I will build again the ruins thereof,
> and I will set it up:
>
> That the residue of men might seek after
> the Lord, and all the Gentiles, upon whom
> my name is called, saith the Lord, who doeth
> all these things (Acts 15:15–17).
>
> In that day will I raise up the tabernacle
> of David that is fallen, and close up the
> breaches thereof; and I will raise up his
> ruins, and I will build it as in the days
> of old.

That they may possess the remnant of Edom,
and of all the heathen, which are called by
my name, saith the Lord that doeth this
(Amos 9:11–12.)

Naturally some controversy continued in some sectors of the church throughout much of the first century, but the scriptural truth on the subject gradually became predominant in the rank and file of the believers. The faith in Christ transcends worldly lineage so that, as Paul stated so simply, "There is neither Jew nor Greek in Christ."

Christology

The controversy about the nature of the church was soon replaced by the controversy over the nature of Christ, or the doctrine of Christology. We have already seen that the apostles wrote against Gnosticism, which taught that Christ was neither fully God nor fully man but some kind of created demi-god. Other false teachings about Christ sprang up and raged for over two hundred years.

It was finally determined that the Bible taught that Christ is 100 percent God, but He is also 100 percent man. We cannot comprehend this concept, it is part of the mystery of God. Furthermore, while Christ is one Person, His divine and human natures are fused together in an everlasting union.

Two major protagonists in this controversy were Arias, who taught that Jesus was not God, and Athanasius, who believed in the deity of Christ. The Scriptures were diligently studied. The church leaders ultimately met in Nicea and concluded that the biblical truth projected the concept of the full deity and humanity of Christ. One of the major developments of this council was the Nicene Creed, which is considered by almost all branches of Christianity to be the pristine statement of basic biblical faith in the Lord.

Soteriology

The Dark Ages passed without much theological debate or controversy, but in the sixteenth century an ethical difference over biblical truth developed. The matter concerned *Soteriology*, or the doctrine of salvation.

The church throughout Europe had become dominated by Rome. There were few if any Bibles available for the people to read. Salvation had become thought of as obedience to church policies, practicing good works, doing penance, and venerating saints and ancient sacred relics.

But a monk named Martin Luther began studying the Scriptures, and he gradually became convinced that the pervasive teaching on salvation was contrary to the biblical sanctions on the subject. He went to Rome to seek guidance from the Mother Church. While he was climbing the stairs that had been brought to Rome from Jerusalem (said to be the stairs from Pilate's judgment hall) a great truth suddenly dawned on him. Paul had said, "The just shall live by faith" (Romans 1:17). Here was the true biblical key to salvation, thought Luther. Faith in Christ alone was the way of salvation, Luther concluded, and he began to write and teach this doctrine.

We should realize that in coming to this conclusion Luther did not invent a new theology but rather rediscovered the original. The Apostle Paul had taught the same thing, but his teaching had been buried under an enormous body of man-made church law and tradition. Luther went forward energetically, nailing his inflammatory "Ninety-five Theses" on the church door in Wittenberg and beginning the process that has come to be known as the Reformation Movement.

For centuries the debate over salvation continued. The result has been that those who embrace the traditional concepts of medieval religion with works, penance, and ecclesiastical obedience in the foreground have tended to gravitate toward the Roman Church with its papal hierarchy; those who concentrated on faith, biblical authority, and individual relationship to God have been oriented toward the various Protestant ministries with their relatively autonomous bodies.

Eschatology

More recently, biblical discussion has turned to the realm of eschatology, or prophecy. The term eschatology literally means knowledge about "the last things," and it is entirely fitting that the church would eventually come to unraveling the complex system of biblical predictions. During the last century or so many have felt that those "last things" were approaching, with reasonably cogent sanctions from the Scriptures.

For most of the centuries of the church age theologians had paid relatively little attention to the details of prophecy. Great volumes on theology were written with only cursory attention to end-time subjects such as Heaven and Hell. This is remarkable because the New Testament writers constantly alluded to the return of Christ and the last days. But the prevailing view of both Catholic and Protestant church bodies was that Christ would ultimately judge the living and the dead and that was the extent of prophetic teaching.

During the nineteenth century theologians began to explore more of what the Bible says about the future, and studied in greater detail the many prophecies in the Old and New Testaments. They discovered, or rediscovered, numerous concepts that had been lost to a great extent for most of the church age, such as the Millennium, the Tribulation, and the Rapture.

The scholars who were willing to depart from church tradition began to write about the coming Millennium, when Christ will return to the earth in person and reign over the world from Jerusalem. This involved the literal fulfillment of many promises that God made to Israel in the Old Testament, including the national restoration of the Jewish people to their ancient homeland. At first, only a handful of Bible scholars, along with some rabbinic teachers, believed in the restoration of Israel. Now that it is a reality, there is still a strong debate in Christian circles as to whether the modern state of Israel is part of the prophetic plan of God or just a humanly contrived event. Our view, of course, is that what we are seeing today is the gathering of the "dry bones" of Israel from the nations of the earth back to the Promised Land as preparation for the return of Christ and national salvation (Ezekiel 36–37).

If the regathering of the Jewish people to Israel in 1948 is a mere coincidence, rather than answering to the host of biblical prophecies about that event, then it is one of the remarkable coincidences of all time. Unprecedented in human history is the return of a nation to its former land, speaking the same language, practicing the same rites and worshiping the same God.

But if there is to be a literal Millenium there would also have to be a literal Tribulation. Students of the Scriptures began to realize that the end-times prophecies of judgment had not been fulfilled during the time of the Roman Empire, as had been previously taught, but were yet to occur. They sought to draw together the dozens of passages that speak of events to come in many parts of the Old and New Testaments and to make a coherent schedule of what is called the Tribulation. Even among those who believe in the coming Tribulation there is much debate about the sequence of events during that awesome time of satanic activity and divine judgment.

Our view, as portrayed in this book, is that the Antichrist will initiate the Tribulation by signing a treaty with Israel, will be catapulted to power through a Russian invasion of Israel, in which Israel will be the surprising victor, and that the Antichrist will ultimately claim to be God and perpetrate the most despicable abomination before God. All of this will culminate in the final war, Armageddon, which Christ will end at His return.

But then there is the question of the Rapture of the Church, a detail of great importance to us who are still living in the Church Age. Will Christ indeed come for His own? If so, will He come before the Tribulation, during it or at the end? Among those who believe in the Millennium and the Tribulation these questions are hotly debated.

Again our view is that the Rapture of the Church is imminent, and that the Lord could return at any moment to take us to glory. But He may well continue to delay His return also. We do not, we cannot, know otherwise, but we live in an ongoing expectation. As the coming of the Lord draws closer, and as events seem to be setting the stage for the end-times developments, it is altogether fitting for the Church to be concerned and interested in these things.

The End of the Age?

We can readily see that the history of the development of doctrine has a logical sequence. When the Church was being formed, the Church was discussed. Now that many feel we are at the end of the age, the ultimate prophecies are being discussed. The Bible is a complex, lengthy and subtle book, and its author is unfathomable. Such discussion throughout the Church Age has given the varied community of believers a hearty vitality and interest in the divine will.

It should be realized that Bible study, like scientific study or any other discipline, has made sweeping advances in modern times. For the majority of the Church Age the Bible was not available to the average church member in a language he could read, and, in point of fact, through much of that time he was advised not to attempt to read it. But with the huge outpouring of vernacular translations in the past few centuries, laymen everywhere have been able to put their minds to the task of achieving real understanding of the biblical message. Progress in biblical doctrine can hardly be referred to as "new discoveries," since there has been no authentically new revelation since John finished the final book of the New Testament. Instead, what has transpired in the way of progress has come about through the diligence of Spirit-led students of God's Word, prayerfully thinking through the original Bible and sharing their findings.

We hope that in this small survey book we too have imparted some useful information. No attempt has been made here to bring forth new truths but rather to elucidate and clarify those which were revealed and have been found. Our prime purpose is less to explain the Bible as to call attention to its leading Character. Old Testament and New, the Messiah of Israel stands at the center of spiritual history. He has always existed and He always will exist. It is up to each one of us to choose to believe in Him or not. If our work here promotes a heightened sense of belief in Jesus Christ, then we have accomplished our ultimate purpose.

We might close by reminding the reader that the findings

of many a well-studied scholar of prophecy indicate that there surely is an end to the Age of Faith, and that salvation by grace will not be available to the race of man forever. If the end of the age is indeed near, then the unbeliever of today can think about no more important a subject than the salvation given freely by the Savior Jesus Christ.

CHRISTIAN HERALD ASSOCIATION AND ITS MINISTRIES

CHRISTIAN HERALD ASSOCIATION, founded in 1878, publishes The Christian Herald Magazine, one of the leading interdenominational religious monthlies in America. Through its wide circulation, it brings inspiring articles and the latest news of religious developments to many families. From the magazine's pages came the initiative for CHRISTIAN HERALD CHILDREN'S HOME and THE BOWERY MISSION, two individually supported not-for-profit corporations.

CHRISTIAN HERALD CHILDREN'S HOME, established in 1894, is the name for a unique and dynamic ministry to disadvantaged children, offering hope and opportunities which would not otherwise be available for reasons of poverty and neglect. The goal is to develop each child's potential and to demonstrate Christian compassion and understanding to children in need.

Mont Lawn is a permanent camp located in Bushkill, Pennsylvania. It is the focal point of a ministry which provides a healthful "vacation with a purpose" to children who without it would be confined to the streets of the city. Up to 1000 children between the ages of 7 and 11 come to Mont Lawn each year.

Christian Herald Children's Home maintains year-round contact with children by means of an *In-City Youth Ministry*. Central to its philosophy is the belief that only through sustained relationships and demonstrated concern can individual lives be truly enriched. Special emphasis is on individual guidance, spiritual and family counseling and tutoring. This follow-up ministry to inner-city children culminates for many in financial assistance toward higher education and career counseling.

THE BOWERY MISSION, located at 227 Bowery, New York City, has since 1879 been reaching out to the lost men on the Bowery, offering them what could be their last chance to rebuild their lives. Every man is fed, clothed and ministered to. Countless numbers have entered the 90-day residential rehabilitation program at the Bowery Mission. A concentrated ministry of counseling, medical care, nutrition therapy, Bible study and Gospel services awakens a man to spiritual renewal within himself.

These ministries are supported solely by the voluntary contributions of individuals and by legacies and bequests. Contributions are tax deductible. Checks should be made out either to CHRISTIAN HERALD CHILDREN'S HOME or to THE BOWERY MISSION.

Administrative Office: 40 Overlook Drive, Chappaqua, New York 10514
Telephone: (914) 769-9000